CODING

GAMES

A COMPREHENSIVE BEGINNERS GUIDE TO LEARN
THE REALMS OF CODING IN GAMES FROM A-Z

ROBERT C. MATTHEWS

Table of Contents

Introduction

The world of game programming is vast and enticing. For many of us, the desire to program games comes from the first time we played one. For others, it's about the developmental challenges and solving puzzles that pop up.

Regardless of why you want to go into the field, game programming has something in store for you. If you're a creative person, then you'll enjoy thinking of the intricate mechanics you can put into your game. If you're more of a problem solver, then you'll enjoy fixing bugs and issues during coding. On the other hand, if you are detail-oriented, you'll enjoy the balancing aspects to ensure your game isn't too easy or too hard.

Many people get into game programming thinking that it'll be a breeze and that all they need to do is think of how things should work and that's it. That is the job of a game designer (although that isn't all they do either.) Game programming means knowing the game inside and out.

If you're expecting an easy job, you won't find it in-game programming. However, if you're fascinated by the inner workings of video games, and are willing to put in the time to master it, then you're looking at one of the most fascinating fields out there.

In this book we'll be going over the expectations of this job and getting you to grips with the basic parts of game programming.

Chapter One

Set Your Expectations

Game programming is vastly different from any other kind of programming. Some of its good parts come from the cutting edge challenges you can come across, as well as the satisfaction of seeing your name run across the credit screen. Furthermore, everyone loves games! Go to any game store and both customers and staff alike will be happy to see you.

If you choose to work for a large company, you'll also get to work with some of the greatest game development kits out there from companies like Valve and Unity. These companies make a lot of tools that can help you bootstrap your game from nothing to an enjoyable experience.

The unfortunate part of game programming is that it can be really difficult work sometimes. You'll face management problems, hardware and operating system changes, as well as how best to ensure your users experience the abstract concept of "fun" consistently.

In this chapter, I'll try to set your expectations of game programming. After it, you'll know whether you really want to go on to be a game programmer as a career.

The Good Part

The jobs within the gaming industry are fast changing, and the field itself is constantly evolving. For example, back when I was starting out with game programming, the dominant language to use was Assembly. Today, you'd be hard-pressed to find a modern game written in it.

There was no such thing as being simply a game programmer in the early days of the gaming industry. You did everything, ranging from the code to the art and game design elements.

Today, you see large companies segmenting the position into very niche areas, for example, you might be specialized for programming game physics or databases.

Back when I was starting out as a game programmer they wore ties, and you would be hard-pressed to find a difference between them and a regular office.

Today, wearing a tie to an interview as a game programmer is no longer the norm. I've even seen people show up in a shirt and flip-flops. With that being said, the industry is even more cutthroat than back then. With the boom that games have achieved, the difference between a mediocre and a good game programmer has become massive.

The industry is also quite secretive, which can be quite fun sometimes. You'll get the chance to experience brand new games years before customers get their hands on them. Though you should expect that most big-name publishers will ask you to sign an NDA so that their secrets aren't accidentally leaked outside.

The best part of working on games, for me at least, is that they are as close to art as they are to science. While writing this book I've put a great deal of thought into why I find this line of work so satisfying despite all the pressure. In the end, I simply loved how well games blend in the art and math together.

This can be best exemplified in things such as character movement. As an end-user, you will notice that the movement feels "off." But as a game programmer, my job was to figure out why exactly it felt that way and fix it.

The art comes from grasping how the natural human movement looks, and the math came in when I needed to put it in the game. It forces the left and right side of your brain to work together, and when they do- it's truly a sight to behold.

Sometimes, the scientifically most sensible approach isn't even the correct one. Sometimes you have to tweak it a little to show the innate imperfections found in human movement, much like an artist would change a facial expression on a portrait.

It's also very fun to work together with designers and take the discussions to and from the lunchroom. "Steve, seriously, we've been over this. The master zombie characters came from planet B831; they're not experiments originating from Earth, that was last week's pitch!"

Personally, I also get a lot of fun out of simply coding. Especially when it's going well, as I'm one of those people that take bugs as a personal insult from the game engine to me. When you start getting into new technologies, such as new consoles and such, then you'll have a lot of fun... and a lot of times when you wish we had just stuck to the simplicity of the NES.

On occasion, you'll find fun in optimization. Maybe you'll crack the puzzle on how to implement an algorithm in a way that your game now runs at 60FPS, an acceptable framerate, rather than looking like a PowerPoint presentation.

It's also very fun whenever I start a new project. When I have to allow everything in my libraries to be refreshed and rewritten. Though being fair, as game development is notorious for harsh deadlines, sometimes you'll have to deal with a few hastily done objects and such.

Though if I had to pick one thing that I love the most about game programming, it would be the freedom it brings. No other kind of programming gives you as much freedom as game programming, partly because it moves so fast.

Gamers Are A Joy

One of the best things about being a game developer is the people playing your game. Working in the game industry, you should be prepared for people to barrage you with questions ranging from "what is your game about?" (you should know this) to "when will it come out?" (you will probably not know this.)

If you're working with a big-name company, there's a solid chance that you won't be able to answer any of these legally. If you're working on Nintendo's next Pokemon game, you'd better bet they won't let you tell anyone what the next set of starters will be.

On the other hand, when you encounter people who enjoyed a game you've made, it's awesome to talk to them. It's always a good feeling when fans buzz about a game you're developing, or when they're already talking about the sequel before you're even back from vacation.

Seeing websites, subreddits, forums, and Wiki pages for a game you helped create is an extremely fulfilling feeling.

Another benefit of being a game programmer is interacting with people aspiring to be you. I always enjoy talking to would-be game programmers that have the talent and willingness to work- like you do since you're reading a whole book about it!

With that being said, these days there's a lot more game development going on outside of big-name studios. Indie games are becoming more and more popular, and some of Steam's best-sellers are indie titles, such as The Binding of Isaac and Darkest Dungeon.

Another sneaky benefit of being a game programmer that you should keep in mind is that you can finally tell your parents that playing all those games did some good in your life.

Make Demos, Not Resumes

The world of game programming is one of practice. You are hired based on what you can do, rather than what you say you can do. A high-quality demo game is a better pitch than a full resume; it may even be better than a degree.

For example, the best game programmer I've ever worked with started out as an amateur. But the man had dedication in spades. By the time I knew what Z-sprites were, he had already rewritten Ultima VII to support them. Let's just say that he got hired very quickly.

Rather than simply working mind-numbing plain programming jobs until you rack up an impressive resume- work on a passion project. It needn't be much; it doesn't have to have the most cutting edge graphics or even be all that good of a game. What clients want to see is that you can make games, not that you can simply code.

The Coworkers

Your coworkers are people that you should really want to like. With that being said, after a couple of 18-hour coding crunches, you'll be a family whether you want it or not. After all, chances are you'll be seeing them more than your family from time to time.

A game development studio is a strange place where programmers, artists, audio composers, and testers all get along...at least until someone messes up. It's also important to note that a lot of your coworkers will be self-taught rather than university educated.

In general, game programming jobs are more suited towards people with varied skills, rather than people with degrees. This isn't to say that self-taught programmers are slackers, or that university graduates lack a certain spark.

If you've got an education in programming, you'll sometimes see them speaking for thirty minutes about an amazing new data structure they came up with... just to find that they're literally describing a B+ tree.

The most rewarding and challenging people to work with are the artists. Personally, I just see them as the other side of programming. They always come up with outlandish ideas, with little clue whether or not you can make it happen.

Rather than brushing them off immediately, think about whether you can do it. Artists are the best at pushing game programmers to their absolute limits. Sometimes, you'll find that you're the happiest about the things you wrote because someone gave you an idea so outlandish you just had to give it a shot.

Animators and programmers tend to have quite an intense relationship as well. Think about it like a balancing act on a rope. The animator needs to ensure that the character looks good at doing what they do. On the other hand, the programmer needs to ensure that they look good and feel responsive to the player.

These two can be quite difficult to combine, but when they're done seamlessly the game really benefits from it, like we can see in fighter games like Skullgirls or Street Fighter.

As an example of this, let's take an issue I had with an animator over jumping. When a player wants to jump, they expect their character to jump up immediately. However, in practice this doesn't look very good, as actual jumps involve wind-ups. So eventually the animator and I settled on a small wind-up time followed by the jump.

Game designers are also a unique bunch of people. Every other part of the game development process can find work in another industry. Game programmers go into programming; animators can go into 2D or 3D work, and composers can make music, etc.

On the other hand, game designers have a lot more of an all-rounder approach. They usually have good knowledge of writing, choreography, and game experience.

Their primary task is to ensure that the game is not only merely works from a technical standpoint, but for them actually to be entertaining to play. They need to always keep in mind the fundamentals that drive players to play and enjoy games.

All of this can lead to some rather peculiar people, which you'll find going from collaborative, friendly people you can easily compromise with, to egomaniacal dictators that want to supervise your every keystroke.

When working with game designers, it's important to keep in mind their vision of the game and ask them questions about it. The ability to interact successfully with game designers is one of the most important soft skills to have as a game programmer.

Audio composers and sound engineers are generally the last part of the game creation process. Usually audio is made after all the content is settled into place. The story tends to be told through voice-overs, and every action characters make tends to have its own sound accompanying it. Sound effects can't really be done before animations are finished, which means that whenever you're late the sound designers have a bit less time.

Finally, there are the game testers. These can be anything from a kid that's still in high school to an educated, trained quality assurance professional. Whichever they are, they are who you rely on to release a game that is a bit more than a buggy mess.

Sometimes, these will be the game designers, however, most of the time they're simply the people that are well aware of the difference between what a fun game feels like and what an "okay" game feels like.

Because of this, you should always value their input, and try your best to fix the bugs that they find (and trust me, there will be bugs.)

Another benefit of working in game development is all the varied and new hardware you'll get to work on. For example, the first games on the 3DS were the first ones to experience stereoscopic 3D rendering.

On the other hand, games like Thief were able to utilize the latest in audio and video technologies available at the time. In the old days of Ultima, the games themselves were pushing on systems so hard that some players would straight up buy a new PC every time a new game came out. Yes, that is the equivalent of paying $3,000 for a game.

A lot of higher budget PC titles are made on hardware which still isn't available to consumers. Getting to play around with the new toys is always fun, and sometimes the publisher will even drop you a free shirt or similar. A good enough developer can even call any hardware company and fetch their developer program. Sure, you might not get free hardware like in the old days, but you still get a lot of cool stuff.

The Hard Bit

Game programming is like any other job in that there are the good bits, the bad bits, and the meh bits you just have to push through. While I may be biased, I would say that game programming is by far the most frustrating job in existence.

Sure, many people will vouch that programming games is the hardest kind of programming out there, but that doesn't even begin to cover it. If you are someone that enjoys challenges you will enjoy this part, but don't worry; there'll be another frustrating part for you to take part in.

It's also worth pointing out that the time pressure is quite insane. It's not rare for game devs to be developing something completely new on a deadline. And by "new" I'm not referring to minor modifications to data structures. I'm talking more about applying theoretical designs for the first time. For example, when looking at Ultima VII, we can see that one of the devs wrote a 32-bit MMS (memory management system) which was rooted in the intel 486 processor flag combined with hardcoded assembly.

You'll notice that there's a lot of press these days when a game release is delayed; however, for me it's more surprising that they get completed in the first place. There's so much technology involved and created here that I'm amazed they can put it out in such short timeframes.

There's more to making a game than mere code; however, if you check out any PC game made recently, you'll notice it's full of DLL and EXE files. Most likely you'll even encounter tons of file extensions you've never seen in your life. Every part of a game comes from a file. Every sound effect you hear when you swing your sword was once a WAV file. Every model and level in the game was part of its own file. Each game is hundreds of these combined.

Bugs And/Or Features

This is an actual bug that happened to me during development: My character was walking, and trees started turning into shovels, and then my character suddenly became a pair of boots. Naturally, the game crashed straight afterward.

That doesn't even sound like a real thing. Seriously, game code can be a real mess. You won't be seeing bugs like that in any other occupation. The code will always be crazy.

Now, you could be thinking about why something so funny is put into the section with downsides. Well... sometimes bugs aren't as amusing. Sometimes games are rushed out so quickly there isn't enough time to fix all the bugs out there.

There's way too much pressure put on developers to make their games ready to test in project management. The heavy volume of bugs found in games these days is an issue the whole industry is battling. The worst of it is that not only is it a logistical nightmare; you're actually encouraged to make it so at most companies.

Thankfully, some bizarre bugs that happen can actually turn into a feature. These are usually the bugs that aren't entirely game-breaking but are difficult to fix. These features are usually pushed under the rug.

The Tools Themselves

The lord and savior of game development, Richard Garriott (creator of the Ultima series) has made a rather apt comparison between the gaming and movie industries. A lot of the time, projects will start by coming up with everything that surrounds them. In the movie industry, that's cameras, techniques, and projectors, while in the gaming industry that's engines.

Sure, you could make an awesome game in, say, Unreal engine, but most commercial endeavors opt for a custom solution instead. Usually, before making the game, you'll be making the tools to make the game.

A lot of games have special editors for different levels, zones, and missions. While Ultima was in development, we'd spend our first year simply writing the editor for the game. The editor was just a tool that allowed us to put in graphics, sounds, and models into the game.

The editor was entirely networked, utilizing TCP and IP to communicate peer-to-peer with everyone involved in the project. It was even possible for multiple programmers to edit the same map at once (though that is no longer impressive.)

The Ultima Online editor was even better, almost looking like a game. Though the older games used simpler technologies, they were good enough for making simpler maps and areas.

The Bad Part

Now, while game development is my favorite job in the world and I wouldn't change it for anything, that doesn't mean it doesn't have its downsides. In this section, we'll be going over those.

There are a lot of things that make game development a constantly changing, fluid, and temperamental beast. There are a variety of different motivators at play whenever a game is made, both internal and external.

The "crunch mode" is the first of these downsides. If you've ever hung out with game devs, you'll have heard them talking about "crunching." This refers to a practice where developers gather into a room, and bash on their keyboards (and occasionally monitors) endlessly until they've finally finished.

While a crunch can leave you feeling happy and accomplished, during one you simply feel like you're about to drop at any point if you aren't fed coffee through an IV.

This is partly due to the fact that the standards you're supposed to meet are constantly changing, and development goals can change in a split second. This is why developers can be heavily put onto the spot sometimes.

System analysis is dedicated to finding out the requirements of your consumers. They'll use software case studies and other research methods months before it's time for you to write even one line of code.

On the other hand, the architecture governing Ultima VIII was entirely planned out within an afternoon by seven people in front of a chalkboard.

Sometimes, the initial design simply isn't fun. Unfortunately, fun isn't something that is easily tweaked. You can make a whole game, just to find out that it isn't fun.

Your only option is to put all your hopes into the original design actually being a fun game to play and pray. Unfortunately, the first playable edition of a game usually sucks. They usually simply leave the player feeling like they lack something.

Sometimes, that means moving a few things around and changing it up. At other times, that can mean drastically changing the design of the whole game. Because of this, the job can be rather stressful.

At first, the map design of Ultima VIII revolved around a hub-and-spoke model. The hub itself was situated in an underground dungeon. From there, the player could go to any map they desired.

After a round of QA testing... we found out the game was simply boring, and the reason was that there was a sparsely populated central map that was little past a maze.

After we reworked the whole thing to include things that players enjoy such as monsters, traps, and puzzles, the central map wound up being one of the most fun elements of the game.

Crunches

Your first project might not force you to crunch, maybe the second won't either, but you'll be toast by the third. Sometimes, the whole project can wind up at a dead-end technologically speaking. This is where it's usually necessary to start completely over.

For example, I got brought in for a complex Mattel project that was intended to enter testing in just two weeks. After taking a look at the code there... I found out they were using Windows GDI. Windows GDI is unable to create texture polygons. This meant that the whole project needed to be rebuilt from scratch.

This included some basic essentials such as a 2D vector animation program. These 5 weeks felt to me more like 15. While the development team was tiny, we all worked up until late into the evening and then dragged ourselves back into office by the next morning. Weekends were a forgotten concept. We probably ground ourselves with 90-100 hour workweeks for that week.

Now, sure, that does sound unreasonable. I'm not going to contest that, but this is a reality of the job. This was only 5 weeks though, which pales in comparison to some of the more crunch heavy companies.

For example, Origin Systems used to have a club called "100 Club." So, how would you gain entry into this club? Well...you would have to work a 100 hour week. If you found yourself within this club, you would have no doubt gone through a round of questioning your life decisions.

As simple math can tell us, a week has 168 hours, and if you sleep 8 hours a day (a luxury in the game programming world) then you are left with 12 hours of free time... for a week.

The schedules at Origin Systems were so hellish that the teams wound up building bunk beds within their company kitchens. Unfortunately, the office of yours truly was found straight across the hall. I was able to see the kitchen and bedroom combo house more people than the local homeless shelter- and these were all well-paid programmers.

A week in, I noticed that the locale was smelling more and more; it appeared as if they forgot to hire a maid service. The management at Origin shut the experiment down soon after that.

Even today, it isn't rare for companies to want you to work really long hours, though they provide you with meals most of the time. These so-called crunch meals are usually food that was ordered and delivered to you. Usually, this is from a place that can just bill the company rather than use credit cards.

In the Origin development team, we soon learned the menu at Jason's Deli by heart. I know parts of the menu even today, as we ate the food almost every night. Their food is good, though I can't bring myself to eat there today.

You might think that crunching will stop as you grow older. Well, at the young age of 38, I found myself crunching in the process of creating the latest installment in the "Thief" series. Trust me, the older you get, the harder it is to keep yourself awake and coding up until late at night. This was intensified as it lasted for weeks upon weeks.

Unfortunately, crunch mode is present in pretty much any modern studio. This is because most publishers simply won't allow games to be released in a manner that would facilitate a simple, 40-hour workweek. If you've ever worked at EA, you should know about one of the biggest scandals in the gaming industry over their crunch times.

While you might think that the scandal stopped such things from occurring, all it meant was that the crunch was outsourced.

You're At The Mercy Of The Seasons

Much like skiing gear, games are a seasonal business. You'll find that games sell a lot less as summer grows near, and a lot more as it passes by you and we get into Christmas time. Now, the only time that a game can be selling well is if you're already done working on it.

On occasion, you'll have the pressure on you before you even start working on the game. If you're working on downloadables, then it's unlikely you'll be getting much revenue unless it's done near the holiday rush. On the other hand, if you're doing a retail title, then you definitely want to get your game onto store shelves as soon as possible.

Now, some publishing companies tackle this differently from others. For example, massive conglomerates like Microsoft have huge manufacturing pipelines, including things ranging from the new Halo installment to the latest edition of Microsoft Office. Heck, I spent time working on a game that was shipping the same month that Windows XP was.

Uncertain Employment

While you're unlikely to find yourself unemployed as a game dev, you're also rather unlikely to find yourself in a situation where you're working with the same set of people for more than say, a year or two. This is because gaming companies are very fond of mass layoffs and will rarely stick with the same employees for more than 2-3 years.

For example, Origin hosted annual Christmas parties. At these parties, employees would be asked to stand up and then sit down for each year that you've worked with them. By the time I was in my sixth year of employment, I was the twelfth most senior employee out of the hundreds we had at the company.

This is extremely common in the industry, although you can find companies that are different in the nature of their products and their company culture, these companies are just a lot harder to find. There are a lot more companies that simply want to stress you out with short schedules and wear their canceled projects as a badge of honor. This type of thing is what took out most of my friends away from the industry.

This also applies to people above you in the corporate chain. The boss you have today is not the same boss that you'll have tomorrow. This is especially true if your boss likes taking risks such as starting up a game studio. You might even find yourself having a former boss as an employee.

Out of all the companies I've worked for, at least half of them no longer exist. There's also a designer at Valve that I've worked with in 3 separate companies.

So, Is It Worth It?

So, now you know the gist of what you should be expecting if you go into this industry. With all of this being said, is it worth it to go into this field? For me, the answer is yes.

There's a weird thing about the way humans work. When we experience something that left us terrified, or if we have a really painful experience, we'll think, "Well, that wasn't *too* horrible, I guess I could do it again!"

Game developers are extremely familiar with this line of thinking. The job is really difficult, and it will do its best to drive you completely insane. The tools you use and the systems you develop for are rapidly changing. There are days where you erase more code than you put in.

By taking three steps forward and following them up with five back, you'll be working very long hours and eating an all you can eat buffet of overtime.

This will get bad. How bad? One day, you'll leave work at 6 PM on a Sunday evening... and you'll feel guilty about it. When the crunch is done, and the routine of your 60-hour workweek is back, you'll be confused as to what to do with all that time.

There will be countless times where you'll think that a simple office job was a better fit for you. But is it? Absolutely not. There are plenty of good things about the job, but there's one that leaves the rest in the dust.

After all the work you put in after your fight with producers, testers, and your coworkers, you'll see your game appear on the shelves at the store. It will be your game in stores. It'll be in a box. On the shelf.

There's nothing like that feeling in the whole wide world. You'll have someone walking up to you and asking, "Hey, I wanted to buy that book...is it any good?" And you'll be able to tell them, "Yeah, it's amazing."

Chapter Two

To Indie or Not to Indie

These days, indie development is getting more and more press in the gaming world. Games like Risk of Rain 2 and The Binding of Isaac are topping the best-selling charts and making some developers question if going for a big-name publisher is even worth it.

The divide is essentially between games like The Witcher 3, Civilization VII, Dishonored, FIFA 2020, and games like Super Meat Boy, Transistor, The Binding of Isaac, or Stardew Valley.

Now, can we say that one group of these games is objectively better than the other group? No, we can't, as both are excellent games that have attained critical and financial success. Even besides that, they're both simply fun.

The first group games aren't all sequels, nor are the games in the 2nd group all stand-alones. With that being said, the 1st group does tend to be significantly more expensive than the second. With their prices being ~$60+optional DLCs, the indies are usually priced closer to $15 or $30.

Now, while we could spend hours talking about how AAA and indie developers differ in a variety of factors here we want to establish which you'd rather work for.

This chapter is intended to set your expectations of independent game development and how to develop a game for a huge company.

What Are The Differences?

Now, why do people separate games into AAA and indie titles in the first place? What is it that creates this two-way split between two seemingly arbitrary groups? Some people might think that it's because the two have entirely different pricing models. However, some AAA titles are cheap or even free (Hearthstone, for example.) On the other hand, there are also indie titles that are expensive.

The next consideration for most people is the game's scale. There again we see that there isn't a difference. There are a lot of indie games with sprawling open worlds filled with content and AAA games with a small world.

In my opinion, the difference is far simpler than either of these- it is size. The size of the company making the games determines everything. Indie games, in my opinion, are those that are made by small companies, usually with less than 30 people, and some are made with companies that have even less than 5 people.

On the flip side, AAA studios (for which I've spent most of my time working) are usually large companies with hundreds of employees at their disposal.

The Team Size Issue

As we've just covered, the company's size is the largest difference between an indie and AAA studio. In the same vein, the team size is also vastly different most of the time. In truth, this is the fact that leads to 90% of the differences between these two processes of game development.

The first difference you'll notice when you switch from one of these to the other is the difference in your position. In an AAA studio, every position is largely filled and specialized; for example, you'll see positions like "engine programmer" or level designer. On the other hand, you won't get to see this if you're working at an indie developer. You'll usually see a position titled "programmer."

There's also a lot more direction in AAA studios. From the moment you're hired, the project lead knows exactly what they want you to do. Meanwhile, if you're working for an indie studio, your role may be a lot less defined, though you'll have a lot more input.

The same way the AAA industry places a lot of value in specializing, indie game development values generalizing your skillset so you can tackle multiple roles. For example, you might be working on networking one day, and be working on the enemy AI the next. This is because small teams are rarely able to cover every position you need for a game, and because of this they look to people that can do a lot of things at once.

This variety is probably the biggest benefit of working with indie development. While you might spend 3 years working at the same game, you'll be working at entirely different aspects of it. This can break up the occasional monotony that can stunt creativity within a project.

Due to this variety, you'll also need to know a lot more than you would working with an AAA game publisher. I'd say indie work is more difficult on the brain, while AAA work taxes your fingers more with all the overtime.

Differences In Funding

This is another obvious difference. A big team will need a lot of money to be funded successfully because there are a lot more people that the company needs to pay. In turn, this also means that games that are made by AAA studios usually have significantly higher development costs.

With that being said, this is also because AAA companies pay their top executives a lot more. You'll see a lot more inequality when it comes to salaries at AAA companies than you will at indie ones. It's not uncommon for a project leader to be making two times what you are at a large company. It isn't rare for the programmer to be making more than the CEO in their budding stages at an indie project.

Indie development also includes fewer people, meaning that there are a lot fewer people to pay. In turn, indie development costs a lot less than it does at big-name companies.

Willingness To Risk

This descends from the above difference. Because AAA development costs a lot more, the risk of it flopping is also a lot greater. If an AAA game flops, the company can wind up losing millions of dollars.

On the other hand, an indie game has nowhere near that amount of risk. Usually, the risk will be rather small. Because of this, indie games are usually a lot more prone to taking risks.

AAA companies like EA get a lot of flak for releasing what is "basically the same game" every year, such as Assassin's Creed, FIFA, and many other sports titles. While I can assure you that no developer at EA would call FIFA18 and FIFA20 "the same game" from a consumer perspective, they are very similar.

This is because, as a large company, EA takes far fewer risks (and it's an outlier even among large companies.) Large companies are much fonder of a "don't fix it if it ain't broke" mentality.

On the other hand, you have developers like Hopoo Games whose first successful game was Risk of Rain. It was a 2D side-scrolling roguelike with powerups and waves of enemies.

For the sequel, an AAA title would most likely add more powerups, larger enemy variety, and maybe improve the characters' models and animations.

What Hopoo games did in Risk of Rain 2 is far beyond that. They made the game 3D for one, which is a huge change from its predecessor. They made it so that aiming is an actual mechanic.

Furthermore, they took risks by taking the roguelike formula and trying to apply it to a 3rd person 3D shooter. As we can see today, this paid out in spades, as the game is one of the hottest selling games on Steam right now.

If this is the kind of risk-taking you enjoy, then you'd probably be better off developing for an indie studio.

With that being said, it's worth noting that taking up risks isn't all positives. Indie companies tend to live from game A to game B. This means that the first game you're working on will have its revenue used to fund the development of their next game.

In turn, this means that if a game flops or doesn't perform well enough, the studio itself could immediately close down.

On the other hand, an AAA studio has more than enough revenue to tank a game not performing too well once or twice, which means that they tend to be much more stable as companies.

There are naturally some exceptions to this, such as CD Projekt Red, which exists in somewhat of a limbo between an indie and AAA company.

Bureaucracy

In an indie game studio, when a decision is to be made, the whole team will gather up and decide on what needs to be done. This can take quite a while, and sometimes friendships are made and broken in these situations.

On the other hand, AAA companies will have executives that might not even play the game make the decision. They will take weeks, or even months before the game has even started development to decide on its direction.

They will do extensive research on the market, taking in current and past trends and analyzing them to see what would go over well with the playerbase. They want to find as many players as possible, so niche titles are out of the question.

Indie developers usually ditch the whole market research aspect. They are usually simply passion projects, and will not shy away from a niche design, even if it alienates some potential customers.

Indie games don't need to sell millions of copies to be profitable; because of this, they can afford to pursue niche titles, as well as take unorthodox design approaches.

There's also a lot less bureaucracy in the world of indie games. Chances are you'll have at most 2-3 people that are straight up above you. On the other hand, in AAA games you'll find that there's a seemingly never-ending chain of executives looking at the back of your head.

Passion

Now, I'm not trying to say that all AAA developers are less passionate; however, as team size increases, you can't help but feel a tiny bit more impartial towards the final result of a project.

If you want to treat game development as a fun job, I suggest you go into AAA development. This is because you can go to work, have some fun, and go back while knowing what to do.

Indie development, on the other hand, is like painting with a tornado. Nobody is sure what everyone else should be doing, but they're united by the currents of passion for making the project a good one.

In an AAA studio, the game is treated more as a product to be put out onto the market. Its purpose is simply to make a profit. It is not to say that there aren't passionate developers in AAA studios; however, their passion must take a back seat.

The Ability To Start Your Own

So, have you ever thought about what it would be like to start the next Blizzard? The next Activision? I think everyone that's into game programming has had these thoughts.

Working for one of them is one way to do this. Who knows, one day you might get to the position of a CEO or a subdivision manager. This is the safer way to get to grips with a company like this and control the kind of games AAA titles are.

Unfortunately, it doesn't have much bearing on your programming skills. You aren't going to get promoted to anywhere past lead programmer without participating in office politics and similar issues.

It's not easy to get to that point either. You can bet that there are hundreds of people gunning for the same seat you are. And each one of them has great skills for it.

Even ignoring that, the importance of connections and the existence of nepotism makes these seats nigh-on unattainable for the great majority of us. Though I wish this were not the case, if you're trying to get there without some truly exceptional people skills, I suggest finding a new goal.

Then there's the other way of getting in charge of such a company- starting as the CEO. In other words, you could start your own gaming company. If your games are good enough, who knows, you might become the next big thing.

For example, CDPR, which is now famous enough to warrant an acronym, started as a small indie studio. Today they're one of the biggest names in gaming, with titles like The Witcher 3 getting game of the year *with a DLC.* And Cyberpunk 2099 is one of the most anticipated titles in all of gaming.

Now, if you're planning to take this road, know it will not be easy. There have been countless indie game dev companies that have sunk in the last 10-20 years.

On this road, you will understand why most AAA companies look at games as a product. It is because it's what they had to do in order to stay afloat in their indie days.

This has the advantage of giving you supreme creative freedom. You can influence the decisions made over the game yourself. This also means that the game will live or die by your decision.

Unfortunately, simply making good games isn't enough to ensure that your company will stay afloat. You will also need to handle marketing in the internet age. This means sponsoring YouTubers, getting advertisements, trying to get good placements on store pages, etc.

And if you aren't good enough in any of these departments, chances are your company will die then and there. The first good game isn't even good enough most of the time.

You'll have to make quite a few games before your company is renowned enough that you're able to feel secure about it.

If you choose to take this route, you'll also have to reexamine what sounds fun and what is actually fun. A certain mechanic can look fun on paper but can be quite dull when played.

All in all, this is a much more involved and stressful approach. If you thought the crunch was bad when you were just a programmer, well now you'll be lucky if you even get to leave the office.

With that being said, there is a light at the end of the tunnel, and if you manage to create a great, enjoyable game, then you might one day be able to join the greats.

Can I Go Between The Two?

This is a question I've been asked quite a few times- is it possible to switch between coding for an AAA company and an indie one?

The answer to this question is both a resounding yes, and a rather timid one. There are a few things to consider if you want to do this. It is generally only advisable if you are either uncertain about which one you want, or if you're planning to amass experience before starting your own game.

The first thing you'll need to take into consideration is how versatile you are. If you aren't interested in multiple facets of game development and are just a programming person, I suggest you stick to big companies. Alternatively, you could gain experience at bigger companies to start your own indie game.

If you've got the work ethic of an Olympian, then you could even have a "side hustle" of sorts.

A side hustle is what many indie games start as. You get a normal job at a regular firm, and work on a personal project on the side. This way, your income isn't tied up to your indie game, and you can focus on making it the best possible product.

After you've got a working prototype, you can pitch it as a Kickstarter, or even publish it as an Early Access title. A game can gain traction like this, and you can slowly switch from working your nine to five to working on your personal game.

I Made My Decision, What's Next?

So, if you've decided on which approach to take, you might get stuck with decision paralysis; after all, there's no tutorial to tell you what to do next.

Fortunately, that's what I'm here for. There are 3 options you could've gone for:

- Getting employed at an AAA developer

- Getting employed by an indie studio

- Starting your own indie game company

In the first case, all you've got to do is do your job! Try to get along with your teammates, of course, but you're already in a pretty enviable position for a game dev. I suggest you try not to shy too far away from office politics, as they can be rather relevant.

Otherwise, try to push for more and more ambitious projects. Since so few people stay at the same company for long, seniority can often be a good argument for a promotion.

In the second case, you'll be having your hands full. Make sure that you've got a proper vision for what you want the game to be. Every line that you write should have a purpose, as you'll be writing thousands of them and don't want to waste time.

Now, it's time to grind. Soon you'll forget the notion of work hours and free time; it'll all meld into one large entity dedicated purely to developing the best project you can. However, it won't be easy, but as long as you focus on picking up as many skills as possible on the job, it'll get easier as time goes on.

By the time you're done with your first game, the second will probably be much easier to do.

In the 3rd case, prepare to live and breathe games for a while. Starting your own game development company is not only an ambitious task, but it is one that a lot of people fail at, and that isn't because they're stupid. The biggest reason for failure is simply a lack of luck or a lack of focus on certain non-programming aspects such as marketing.

Chapter Three

Choosing A Language And
Starting To Program

As you know, games are made using programming languages. These are special languages made so that a compiler can understand them and then translate them into binary for the computer to listen to your instructions.

There are a great many languages in the world of programming, so choosing one to start with can be rather daunting for many beginners. You'll often see languages like C# or Java being recommended; however, these are rather difficult and are far removed from our routine understanding of language.

A good thing about programming languages is that once you know one very well, it's easy to switch to others, as they all work with the same underlying principles.

For the sake of this, and for the sake of easy browser development and general ease of use, we've chosen to use ruby.

Why Ruby?

You'll always find people pushing you to learn a statically typed language such as C++ or similar in game development. Saying how they're the best and that while they may have a steep "learning curve" once you get the hang of them, you're set.

While this may be true, that learning curve is more of a cliff. In fact, starting with a language like that is the easiest way to give up on being a game programmer forever, as they are simply put: boring.

People might even suggest that you go with a ready-made platform such as Unity. This has the downside that you aren't really able to learn how to program, only how to use your platform of choice.

In the end, I settled on ruby for this book. You'll hear a lot of programmers tell you that there's little reason to make a full game through Ruby. After all, all the casual games are generally designed for mobile platforms, while desktop games are usually made with more serious gamers in mind.

With that being said, we aren't going to be making a 3D MMORPG to rival the likes of WoW. Those things you might work on if you end up working at a huge company. As a learning project, we'll be learning something much more akin to the early days of Nintendo games.

Though those games look fairly simple today, you'll soon find that they're actually quite challenging to make, even with the technology at our disposal today. The reason why we don't go mobile and develop for desktops instead is the resurgence of 2D and 16-bit games. There are more and more games on the market today that are trying to capture that old-school feel. Therefore, a slower language such as Ruby doesn't have anywhere near as many downsides.

The biggest advantage of Ruby is that it's simple and easy to learn. You won't need to dedicate years of your life in order to understand it. In fact, I'll guide you through simple Ruby programming in this book. It would be ideal if you also learn some Ruby on the side, as we'll mainly be focusing on the libraries used here, rather than giving you a whole Ruby tutorial (as that's a whole other book.)

What Will We Begin With

This is the question that you should begin with every time you start making a game. You need to have a detailed plan of what exactly you want to build. If you start with a simple concept and keep pushing, soon enough you'll have way too many features to develop them all.

If you've programmed before, you'll already know how to make a game of Tic Tac Toe, and that's the kind of goal you want. You don't want a vague set of characteristics; instead, you want a streamlined outline of your game.

First, let's start with the graphics that we'll be making. We'll rule out 3D graphics immediately for a trifecta of reasons:

1. It needlessly increases the complexity and scope of the game itself.

2. It's quite difficult to optimize 3D graphics in Ruby.

3. If you want to program with 3D graphics, you'll need to get a new book that's a couple of times this size.

So, we'll be going with 2D graphics, but what kind of 2D will it be? Once again, we narrow it down to a few prime candidates:

1. A parallel Projection game, a la Chrono Trigger.

2. A Top-Down game, such as the first games of the Legend of Zelda series.

3. A side scroller such as the first entries of the Castlevania series.

Now, parallel projection is the most difficult of these and is well showcased in games such as Fallout 2. The issue with it is that it requires detailed art to look decent, so we would have a rather difficult time if we began with it.

A top-down view gives you a lot of freedom, and you can explore a lot of directions in the game. It doesn't require too much detail, as things tend to look fairly simple from above.

Finally, side scrollers such as Super Mario Bros are a bit tricky to get right, as they involve stuff like jumping. However, there isn't too much room to explore, as you can only go from left to right (or right to left.)

If we go with the top-down perspective, then we'll have a shot at making the world of our game vast, with a lot of areas to explore. Simple graphics and mechanics are exactly what we need.

If we go with a side scroller, we have less content that we need to make. However, we must pay much more attention to animations and physics, and we don't want that.

The Gosu Library

Now, many beginner game programmers ask themselves if they should implement every element of the game themselves or use some basic boilerplates with a few of the most common functions built-in.

The answer to this is that it depends, sometimes it can be worth it to develop the whole platform yourself. However, this isn't one of those times. Instead of teaching you how to implement everything in the game by hard-coding it, we'll use some existing libraries.

The most important issue about implementing everything yourself is that if you aren't already experienced, chances are you'll just reimplement a game library that already exists out there. There won't be much delay before you've reached the point of needing an interface to get your graphics in order.

Then let's say you want to port the game to Linux. Would you rather re-make the game, or have the library do it for you?

The good news about using a library is that we'll be able to finish in a relatively timely manner. If you're fast, you could wind up with your first game in as little as a week. Then even after we've finished, you'll be able to port your new game to other operating systems such as Mac and Linux.

Now, the best library to use, in my opinion, is Gosu. It's simply that far ahead the rest of the Ruby game development libraries. It also has a wide, blossoming community in case you need help in the future.

You can find the instructions on how to install the Gosu game library on their website.

What Kind Of Game Will We Make?

So, choosing the theme for your game is a crucial aspect of making it. The theme should be something that you enjoy, and still something that wouldn't push the mechanics too far out there, so you'll be able to finish it.

For example, I've probably started at least 5-6 efforts to make a MMORPG with a small studio. Guess how each one of these has ended up? Catastrophic failure. Sometimes it isn't even an issue on the programming end. The graphics are also crucial, as is extensive marketing and the purchase of server space.

Sure, I'd love to make a game where people can run around a vast game world, fighting other players as they see fit and incorporating some mechanics such as free-for-all loot and similar. Despite that, I find myself making simpler games these days.

These are games that are simpler to make and play; however, I can actually finish them, instead of leaving them in development hell.

So, now that we've got our expectations set, I've decided on an appropriately challenging first project for us.

It is a multi-directional shooter arcade game. In this game, you'll take control of a simple spaceship and then roam around the game area trying to kill as many aliens without them returning the favor.

Now, you might be thinking, isn't this basically Alien Invaders? Yes, it is. We'll be implementing that idea with a couple of our twists as our first game. It'll be fun, grueling, and you'll be fighting with bugs before you know it!

We'll be using a subset of graphics which are provided for free by Csaba Felvegi.

I also suggest you get a basic graphics editing program such as GIMP so that you can edit the sprites whenever you want (and you will want to do that.)

Saying Hello In Gosu

As all programming tutorials begin, we'll start with a simple hello world program in Gosu. It should look like this:

```
1 require 'gosu'

2

3 class GameWindow < Gosu::Window
```

```
4   def initialize( (width=320, height=240, fullscreen=false)

5   super

6   self. caption = 'Hello'

7   @message = Gosu::Image.. from_text(

8       self, Hey Everyone! This Is My First Gosu Program!',
Gosu.default_font_name, 30)

9 end

10

11  def draw

12   @message.draw(12, 12, 0)

13  end

14 end

15

16 window = GameWindow.new

17 window.show
```

Try running this code. You should see a message pop up with "Hey Everyone! This Is My First Gosu Program!"

Now, let's try to analyze what we've done here.

First, we'll extend Gosu::Window using our own class, which we'll call appropriately GameWindow. We'll initialize it as a window 320x240 pixels in size. This way, the graphics don't get too stretched over the player's screen.

We take the super, width, height, and full-screen parameters from the Gosu::Window class, and put them in our own GameWindow class.

Afterward, we'll want to set a caption to our window. With the @message instance variable, we will generate an image from the text "Hey Everyone! This Is My First Gosu Program!" by using Gosu::Image.from_text.

Here we want to override the Gosu::Window#draw method, as it wants to redraw our game window. In the method, we'll want to use the draw command on the variable @message. Then, we'll give a set of x and y coordinates, which we'll arbitrarily set to 12. The depth or z coordinate remains at 0.

Screen Coordinates And Moving Stuff Using The Keyboard

As most libraries do, Gosu will treat x as the horizontal axis, while y and z are treated as the vertical and depth axis, respectively.

x and y get measured using pixels, and the z value is a number relative to these two, which by itself doesn't affect anything.

Gosu's coordinate system's origin lies on the pixel at the top left corner of our screen. Its coordinates are 0:0.

The z value is useful when 2 things overlap with one another. Say you want a player to be able to run over a powerup. When you put the player's z value higher than the powerup, the player gets placed "above" it.

For every Gosu game, there'll be a Gosu::Window subclass. This subclass overrides all other callback methods. Whenever you call the method: window.show() then Gosu goes through the main loop. The callbacks are plentiful, and you can find them on Gosu's GitHub.

Let's Start Moving

Now, we'll start modifying our first program in order to move things on the screen around. The code I'm about to show you will print the given coordinates of a message, as well as how many times the screen you see was redrawn with Gosu. We'll also incorporate a basic feature-you'll be able to exit the program by pressing "Esc."

```
1 require 'gosu'
2
3 class GameWindow < Gosu::Window
4   def initialize(width=320, height=240, fullscreen=false)
5     super
6     self.caption = 'This Is My Movement'
7     @x = @y = 11
8     @draws = 0
9     @buttons_down = 0
10  end
11
12  def update
13    @x -= 1 if button_down?(Gosu::KbLeft)
14    @x += 1 if button_down?(Gosu::KbRight)
```

```ruby
15    @y -= 1 if button_down?(Gosu::KbUp)
16    @y += 1 if button_down?(Gosu::KbDown)
17  end
18
19  def button_down(id)
20    close if id == Gosu::KbEscape
21    @buttons_down += 1
22  end
23
24  def button_up(id)
25    @buttons_down -= 1
26  end
27
28  def needs_redraw?
29    @draws == 0 || @buttons_down > 0
30  end
31
32  def draw
33    @draws += 1
34    @message = Gosu::Image.from_text(
35      self, info, Gosu.default_font_name, 12)
36    @message.draw(@x, @y, 0)
37  end
```

```
38
39  private
40
41  def info
42    "[x:#{@x};y:#{@y};draws:#{@draws}]"
43  end
44 end
45
46 window = GameWindow.new
47 window.show
```

Try running it! You'll see a message printed out that you'll be able to move around using the arrow keys.

We use the GosuKb method in order to declare a keyboard input. Each of the keys on the keyboard responds to a separate GosuKb method.

Chapter Four

Time To Start Properly

In this chapter, we'll start and finish your first game. You've learned the basics of Gosu, and we'll go a bit more into that. We'll also go over some places where you can get cool looking graphics for your projects for free. After all, you don't want to be paying for your practice runs.

So, let us begin:

First, we're going to create a simple Rails gem. Its name will be "ShootyShoot"

    user@computer:~$ bundle gem shootyshoot

This will create a basic structure for us:

    +-- lib

    +-- spaceship_game

       +-- version.rb

    +-- spaceship_game.rb

    +-- bin

    Gemfile

    Rakefile

README.md

spaceship_game.gemspec

To store all the assets, we'll use, we will incorporate more folders into the project. The first of which will be the folder for all of our assets. Within it, we'll have a complex composition of folders somewhat reminiscent of this:

```
assets
+-- fixtures
  +-- sound.wav
  +-- music.wav
  +-- ...
+-- fonts
  +-- custom_font.svg
+-- images
 +-- backgrounds
  +-- sprites
  ...
+-- lib
+-- shootyshoot
  +-- version.rb
+-- shootyshoot.rb
+-- bin
Gemfile
```

Rakefile

README.md

...

shootyshoot.gemspec

We can get all the graphics that we're going to use in this project from http://opengameart.org/. You'll notice that most of these aren't quite the cutting edge graphics that you'll see in most AAA titles. However, you also don't have to pay for them, and there's plenty for any kind of project you might want to start.

Now then, as we've said, any Gosu project will begin with a class deriving from Gosu::Window. The smallest thing we can make is something like this:

```ruby
require 'gosu'
class GameWindow < Gosu::Window
  def initialize
    super 330, 330
    self.caption = "The Smallest Thing"
  end

  def update
  end

  def draw
```

```
end

end

window = GameWindow.new

window.show
```

First, we initialize the base class, which is always Gosu::Window. Afterward, we use our parameters to make the window 330x330 pixels. Finally, we caption the window (the caption is what you see on its title bar.) as "The Smallest Thing." Finally, you can make the window go full screen fairly simply, all you need to do is enter ":fullscreen=>true" after you've inputted its width and length.

The update() and draw() methods are overrides of the Gosu::Window method. update() is, by default, used (or in Ruby jargon: called) 60 times per second to ensure that your game can run at least 60FPS. This part will contain most of your game's logic, such as collisions, movement, and similar.

draw() usually comes after this and is called whenever we need the window to be re-drawn for any other reason. In case that the FPS of your game gets low, this is the method that you should blame. When developing, seek to minimize the number of times that you call this method.

Afterward, we will use the show() method, which is tasked with actually showing the player what is going on the screen.

Finally, the close() method is used to close the game itself.

Adding Imagery

```ruby
require 'gosu'
class GameWindow < Gosu::Window
  def initialize
    super 330,330
    self.caption = "Our First Unholy Creation"
    @background_image = Gosu::Image.new("where/your_image.png", :tileable => true)
  end
  def update
  end
  def draw
    @background_image.draw(0, 0, 0)
  end
end
window = GameWindow.new
window.show
```

This is the first step that we'll need to take before we add in images. The Gosu::Image#initialize method will take in two arguments. These will be the name of your file, and your options hash if there is any.

The :tileable => true command is used to say that the images which we'll put in are background images. These are the tiles that our spaceship will fly over.

The Gosu Image method takes the name and an options hash of any file. You can then set the image as a tile or not by using :tileable => true to create a background tile.

So, as you remember, the draw() method is used to draw everything, so we use it in order to create our background image.

Players Need To Move

Now, as you may notice, our current game can't let you move. As we've already learned how to take keyboard inputs, take a look at the following code;

```ruby
class Ship
  def initialize
    @image = Gosu::Image.new("your_picture.bmp")
    @x = @y = @vel_x = @vel_y = @angle = 0.0
    @score = 0
  end


  def warp(x, y)
    @x, @y = x, y
  end


  def left_turn
    @angle -= 5
  end
```

```ruby
def right_turn
  @angle += 5
end

def accelerate
  @vel_x += Gosu::offset_x(@angle, 0.4)
  @vel_y += Gosu::offset_y(@angle, 0.4)
end

def moving
  @x += @vel_x
  @y += @vel_y
  @x %= 330
  @y %= 330

  @vel_x *= 0.89
  @vel_y *= 0.89
end

def draw
  @image.draw_rot(@x, @y, 1, @angle)
end
end
```

Let's take a look. Ship#accelerate takes what we've all hated in high school and uses it for game development. The offsetx/y functions are almost the same as what you could use sine or cosine for. Let's take an example. If we had something that moves 50 pixels on an angle of 20 degrees, then the distance it moves would be offset_x(50,20) horizontally, as well as an offset_y(50,20) vertically.

Now, since the origin of our coordinate system being at the upper left corner is quite unintuitive, we use the draw_rot method to put the center of the image at (x,y) coordinates.

Our player will be drawn with their z coordinate as 1, which will make them go over the background.

Let's Use That Class

```
class GameWindow < Gosu::Window
  def initialize
    super 330,330
    self.caption = "Spaceship Game"

    @background_image = Gosu::Image.new("Location.png",
:tileable => true)

    @player = Ship.new
    @player.warp(160, 120)
  end
```

```ruby
def update
  if Gosu::button_down? Gosu::KbLeft or Gosu::button_down?
  Gosu::GpLeft then
    @player.turn_left
  end
  if Gosu::button_down? Gosu::KbRight or
  Gosu::button_down? Gosu::GpRight then
    @player.turn_right
  end
  if Gosu::button_down? Gosu::KbUp or Gosu::button_down?
  Gosu::GpButton0 then
    @player.accelerate
  end
  @player.move
end

def draw
  @player.draw
  @background_image.draw(0, 0, 0);
end

def button_down(id)
  if id == Gosu::KbEscape
```

```
      close
    end
   end
 end
 window = GameWindow.new
 window.show
```

Now, the Gosu::Window function gives you two member functions you can use, which are used to be overridden. These are the button_down(id) and button_up(id). Both of these are used to obtain feedback based on whether buttons are pushed down. The update() member functions are used in order to change things around when these parameters are changed.

Adding Sound And Text

A game isn't a game without sound effects and pop-up text telling you whenever you power up a little more. With Gosu, we could pull that off like so:

Now let me show you an example of adding additional fonts to our game using the Gosu library.

```
 class Player
  attr_reader :score
  def initialize
   @font = Gosu::Font.new(30)
   @image = Gosu::Image.new("any_media.bmp")
```

```
@beep = Gosu::Sample.new("any_media_sound.wav")
@x = @y = @vel_x = @vel_y = @angle = 0.0
@score = 0
end
# You can put some code to trigger it here
def collecting_stuff(stuff)
  stuff.reject! do |stuff|
    if Gosu::distance(@x, @y, star.x, star.y) < 20then
      @score += 5
      @any_media_sound.play
      true
    else
      false
    end
  end
end
end
```

Now you've got a system that plays a sound of your choosing whenever you pick up something that you've chosen. In the code, we've named it "stuff" and there is"any_media" written for any place where you've got to add your own.

Tying It All Together

Now, after you've tried all of these code samples separately, you'll still need to delve a bit deeper in order to put all of them together.

The essential idea of Gosu game development is that you need to make a class for each of the resources you've got in your game, such as the windows, sprites, players, etc. You do this in the main class of your project (for me that is lib/spaceship_game.rb) once you've got that, you should require all the files, and make it do something like this:

```ruby
require "spaceship_game/version"
require "spaceship_game/sprites"
require "spaceship_game/bullets"
require "spaceship_game/ships"
require "spaceship_game/enemies"
require "spaceship_game/game"
module SpaceshipGame
  def self.init
    begin
      $game = SpaceshipGame::Game.new
      $game.begin!
    rescue Interrupt => e
      puts "This is an error message...looks like someone messed up."
    end
  end
end
SpaceshipGame.init
```

After this, you want to make a bin folder such as bin/spaceship_game.rb where you'll execute the game itself. Use this code for that:

```
#!/usr/bin/env ruby
ENV['BUNDLE_GEMFILE'] ||=
File.expand_path('yourpath/yourpath/Gemfile', nameofyourfile)
require 'bundle/setup'
require_relative "../lib/spaceship_game.rb"
```

This last file needs to be an executable file.

When you're done with this, run your basic game! That is one of the simplest games you could make in Gosu. However, you've made it yourself.

Something A Little Different

Now, let's set apart Gosu for a second, and take a look at text-based RPG's. These are often called MUDs. They are also multiplayer, allowing multiple people to coexist in the same game world.

Creating a MUD is a great test of your game dev capabilities. It involves not only making a story but also creating gameplay out of a simple text. In my opinion, if you can create a fun MUD adventure, then you've got all you need in order to become a good game designer.

So, how does one go about creating a MUD? Well, here's a relatively simple version of one:

```ruby
require 'ruby_mud'
# Controllers are used to define all the actions in the game,
# The server establishes new connections by default
# in OurServer::DefaultController.
class OurServer::DefaultController
  # The on_start function will always be called when someone
inputs a controller.
  #
  def on_start
    # You can use send_text to send messages.
    send_text "Hi! Here are the commands you have in this
MUD"
    send_text "TIME  : Check out what time it is."
    send_text "SAY   : Speak to people."
    send_text "SECRET: Get yourself to a secret place."
    send_text "QUIT  : Stop playing the game."
  end
#Security makes it so you have to whitelist all user-available
commands
  def allowed_methods
    super + ['time', 'secret', 'say'] # Quit is always available`
  end
  # After a command, user input gets defined via `params`.
  def say
```

```ruby
    send_text "You spoke, saying: #{params}"
  end
  def time
    send_text "Oh, you want to know the time? Well it's
#{Time.now} silly"
  end
  #People go to different menus by using transfer_to
  def secret
    transfer_to PokerRoom # This defines the poker room.
  end
end
# An example of another controller / sub-game / menu.
class PokerPlay< OurServer::AbstractController # controllers
are inherited.
  def on_start
send_text You find yourself in a shadowy room, surrounded by
poker cards and a figure stands in front of you. You can't quite
discern their face. However, they are holding a sign which says,
"would you like to play some poker?!'
    send_text 'Type DEAL to get a hand of cards.'
  end
  def allowed_methods
    ['quit', 'deal']
  end
```

```ruby
    def deal
      send_text 'Poker? Who still plays poker? WE'RE ROLLING
    DICE'
      send_text "Your dice came up to #{rand(5)+1}."
    end
  end
  server = MudServer.new '0.0.0.0', '4321'
  server.start # Accepts any incoming connections
  puts 'Click enter if you want to leave.'
  server.stop if gets.chomp
```

Now, can you make an interesting story like this? Can a game like this even have interesting gameplay? These are some game design elements which can be rather hard to define, so we'll be going over that in the next chapter.

After it, we'll proceed to create another simple game. This time, we'll try to combine all the knowledge you've got so far. Instead of me giving you code, and you just understanding it, I'll be giving you exercises to fulfill.

But for now, be content with just looking at the code above. It's fairly simple, but also quite powerful. Don't consider it simply an outdated relic of the past. Many of the same principles that apply to coding a MUD like this apply to coding a more modern RPG.

Don't discard the value that creating a game like this can bring to you. Try expanding upon it. Maybe try making a simple combat system within it?

If you'd like to continue upon the path of using Ruby to create simple RPG's then I suggest you take a look at chapter seven, where we check out RPG Maker, one of the easiest ways to create a 2D RPG out there.

Chapter Five

Making The Game Fun

In this chapter, we'll take a small break from programming to help everything you've learned sink in. Instead, we'll be taking a look at game design elements. We will be looking at ways to not only make your game work properly, but also for it to be entertaining for the player. Fundamentally, that's the biggest difference between a game and a simple app- a game needs to be fun to play.

Now, it's notable that you might not necessarily need to know these practices at every game programming job out there. Some might just want you to sit down and do your job; however, even at that kind of company, there's still value to be gained from knowing how to make a game properly. You can make comments at company meetings and create better code with fun in mind.

If you know these things, you'll have a much easier time following the vision of game designers, as well as giving them useful feedback on their ideas. So, with that being said, let's dig into some of the biggest game design mistakes you can make.

1. Having the player lose off-screen

Falls from glory can be fun to watch. Sometimes, it's fun to watch a former god bring back the power that they lost. With that being said, keep this to the beginning of the game.

This might sound familiar to you: You're at the top of the world, enemies are falling by the dozen left and right. You've got a shotgun and a full bag of ammo. Hordes are coming straight at you, and you're mowing them all down. Then suddenly, a cinematic starts.

The main villain starts wailing on you. All the skills you would've had if you were controlling your character are rendered irrelevant as they quickly lose, without you being able to do anything about it.

This is bad design (especially in combat-focused games) because it ruins the power fantasy that you have carefully crafted for the player. Note that this doesn't apply only to combat games; forcing the player to lose without their involvement in the middle of the game is not a good idea and won't win you any brownie points.

Forcing combat where it doesn't belong

We all love combat. Fighting in games is so prevalent that there are whole genres dedicated to beating people up. Heck, MOBA's are essentially just one large fight.

With that being said, that doesn't mean every game needs combat. Some games are played quite differently. For example, one of the biggest hits of 2020, Animal Crossing: New Leaf doesn't include any combat. The height of violence within the game is capturing a bug in a net!

Despite that, the game has succeeded in dominating the international market due to its cute aesthetic and excellent customization. This game's popularity is one of the biggest reasons why the Nintendo Switch was sold out for a solid month.

3. Unskippable Story Snippets

Story snippets, whether they be dialogue or cutscenes, are great- they're a portal into your game's story, and you should pay close attention that you make them fun and entertaining for the player. However, some players simply don't care.

There are gamers out there that play games exclusively for the gameplay. For cutscenes, we have films and for dialogue, we have novels. In the end, the only thing separating games from these two forms of media is gameplay, so it isn't surprising some people come for it.

This isn't to say that you shouldn't *make* a story. Heck, SuperGiant Games has essentially made their whole studio based on putting stories and gameplay together. With that being said, you should make sure that those players that don't care about it don't have to experience it.

4. Forgetting to adjust for players with disabilities

Almost 5% of the worldwide population is colorblind. If you factor in the fact that colorblindness is more common in men (who are more likely to play games) you'll find that 5-7% of your potential player base is colorblind.

If you forget to include a colorblind setting in your game, you will be alienating those players from your game. It doesn't even take a lot of effort just to have a setting that changes a few color palettes.

The same goes for deaf players. Your game shouldn't have exclusively audio effects. Ensure that when the audio is playing, something is happening on screen as well that a deaf player can spot.

5. Unintuitive Crafting

Crafting systems are extremely popular these days. With more and more games incorporating more and more intricate crafting systems, it's more important than ever to ensure yours is up to par.

Sure, some players like to find out recipes through experimenting with a variety of different ingredients. On the other hand, most players don't want to do this. Your players will then go online and seek answers on the internet. Not only is it irritating to be constantly alt-tabbing out of the game, it also lowers your player's playtime. Having an option for an in-game glossary of all crafting ingredients is an easy way to avoid this. You could also have an option that disables it for the players that want to experiment.

6. Repetitive Play Patterns

This is a sin many new roguelikes are fond of committing. Fighting a horde of 100 goblins alone might be fun the first three or four times; however, after that it simply becomes tedious.

This applies to pretty much everything. You don't want your players to be seeing the same things too many times. Common animations should have an option to toggle them off. At some point, it simply becomes tedious to look at.

This is even worse for games designed to be played repeatedly, such as roguelikes or RPG's with many endings. These games have to ensure that not only is their core gameplay addictive and fun, but that they have enough varied challenges that the player won't encounter the same one a hundred times.

7. Having "Are You Sure?" messages you can't disable

You'll find that a lot of these can simply be boiled down to "don't make your player experience tedious things." We've all played a game or two that showed us a warning before we wanted to do something too many times.

Some games simply seem to think that gamers have no control over their bodies. My mouse hand has never gone crazy and started clicking randomly across the screen. If you want to include a box that asks your player whether they want to do something, simply include a "don't ask again" box they can tick.

For example, this is very common when you click to start a new game on a game that has a single save file (by the way, you shouldn't have a single save file.) You might be thinking there's nobody who wants to play a new game so many times that they get annoyed by that. However, speedrunners would heavily disagree with you.

8. Switching the order of "Continue" and "New Game."

Continue always goes first. This is a fairly small issue, however, it's easy to fix and might help you retain an extra 1-2% of players. The chances are that your player is itching to play by the time they've sat through the intro consisting of 5 million different publisher/ manufacturer logos. Now, if they press the first thing that pops up, and that erases their save...how likely are they to press your game's shortcut again?

9. Not paying enough attention to map design

The best maps out there are those that help the player get from A to B without expending too much effort, while still having ample room for them to explore. If you've designed your game world well, then every step the player takes in it will add to their journey.

If you design your map poorly, then every step they take they will be asking themselves "where the hell is this place." And it can leave them itching ever so close to the "Quit" button.

As a case of this, let's look at the Dark Souls series. The first Dark Souls game is quite comfortably one of the best games ever made. It has an excellent world structure, as well as a sophisticated and inspired map design. Every zone seamlessly transitions into the next; this makes the world of Lordran feel real, even though it is populated by eldritch horrors, monsters, and people slinging spells all around.

On the other hand, Dark Souls 2, while being a good game, fails at this. Don't get me wrong; the individual locations are well-designed by themselves. However, when you incorporate them into a whole, they feel disjunct, almost as if they were at war with themselves. We find the most punctuated example of this in the difference between Earthen Peak and the Iron Keep. Here, you start by going through a complex labyrinth of windmills and tunnels filled with poison, only to wind up at a castle encircled by lava.

10. Not Considering Savegames

If you have your save games tied to locations, there better be a reason for it. Returning to the Dark Souls example, it has savegame locations because it is a game that relishes in being difficult.

If you aren't planning something like this, you want the player to have the ability to save as often as possible. While saving amidst an important event can spell trouble from the programming standpoint, nothing is stopping you from letting the player save when idle in the game world.

11. NPCs the player needs to follow, but they are either exceedingly slow or fast

This is one of the few things that can make me put down an otherwise great game. If I were to rule the world for a day, all of these people would get capital punishment.

When making a "follow quest" which is basically just a quest where the player needs to follow an NPC throughout the game world in search of something, ensure that they are equally matched in speed.

If the player is blitzing past the NPC, then they'll be frustrated having to wait for them to come back. If the NPC is faster than the player, they'll constantly have to play catchup and wonder what they're doing wrong.

Why can't the woman that you rescue out of the Spider Queen's deadly embrace in Diablo 3 simply walk at a pace faster than a starfish throughout the game world? Who knows, but I know the game got a few negative reviews on Steam because of it.

12. Having an "Exit" button that doesn't actually leave the game

If your player presses a button that says "Exit," "Quit," or the like, then they expect to be greeted by their desktop next. They don't expect the game to go to the main menu and wait for them to exit yet again. This is even worse coupled with screens that ask you if you're sure you want to leave the game.

They clicked "Exit" they're sure they want to get to other things. Don't make players resort to the task manager or the like in order to take a break from your game.

13. Weird difficulty curves

A game should start at a set difficulty, and then either maintain it or get harder as the time goes on. If the game stays the same difficulty, you should expect your players to get through endgame content easily.

Instead, if you make the game get progressively harder, then the game will remain challenging for as long as your player is getting better. You should usually ensure that the game is getting harder a bit slower because you still want your player to have that rewarding feeling.

However, what you don't want is for the game to alternate between being easy and hard at seemingly random intervals. Doing this leaves the player dissatisfied and not knowing whether they're getting better.

14. Using weird perspectives or angles

This sin is doubly true for jumping. For example, the jumping in the Assassin's Creed series is tied to the relative camera position of our main character. This can sometimes lead to extremely agitating moments. In moments like pillar hopping challengers, all you can do is pray that you're getting the jump right. You also have to go around the pillar awkwardly so that you make sure you're aligned.

And then you press jump, only for your character to backflip into a gaping hole in the ground. Checking how basic mechanics like jumping feel is integral to every game design process.

Know that your players will experience every one of your hiccups in these areas and not understand the 100's of hours you spent making the game.

Also, using a non-standard perspective can be rather off-putting for many gamers. Even using a non-standard perspective for the genre is rather risky. For example, the God-focused MOBA Smite might have become a bit more popular had it adopted the same camera angles that its cousins League of Legends and DOTA 2 use.

So, What Should I Do Then

In this section, we'll be going over some things you should be doing whenever you're making a game. As well as some best practices and things to keep in mind.

Note that all of this can be changed. The game industry is much like fashion; some things that I might think are absolutely atrocious right now might be in vogue by 2025.

Instead of holding yourself to the letter of the word, try to keep in mind the spirit in which they were intended, and the time they were written.

1. Find your biggest selling point

You might think that the gameplay, the story, the characters, and every element of your game is perfect. Despite this, you should find one of these elements and ensure that you perfect it.

This is your game's "hook" and its biggest selling point. For example, Darkest Dungeon has deep, intricate mechanics, an excellent story, and even fun characters! Despite all that, most trailers are focused on the eldritch, dark atmosphere the game provides, while innovating with mechanics.

Finding a hook doesn't mean you should throw everything else away. Rather, it helps you focus on what the best parts of your game are.

2. Don't ignore sound design

Games being fun is simply irrational. It's like the enjoyment of any other art form; there's no logical reason for it. However, there are things you can do to ensure that your game is easier to enjoy.

Making the sound design in your game better will make your players significantly more engaged with the game. While they might not even consciously notice the songs and SFX effects in the game, their subconscious will pick them up.

Returning to the example of Darkest Dungeon, a good chunk of the game's fame comes from a rather mundane-looking fact: the narrator is great. That might seem like a small thing, but when you hear the narrator say "Barbaric rage and unrelenting savagery make for a powerful ally" then you find that it's all been worth it.

3.   Ensure your controls are intuitive

There are some unwritten rules of game design. Such as WASD being used for moving up, left, down, and right respectively. If your control scheme was instead TFGH, then the player will simply feel like something is off.

Ignoring these conventions is a surefire way to alienate a portion of your playerbase. Furthermore, even if you're already fulfilling this, it's never a bad idea to let the player change their controls however they want.

4.   Don't make the AI too stupid... or too smart

This is a weird notch to turn. It's extremely easy to make the AI of any game entirely too stupid for its own good, in the same vein, usually it's very easy to make the AI so good it simply stomps the human player.

As an example of this, let's look at Pong. In Pong, it's easy to make an AI that will literally never lose to a human player. To compensate for this, delays are used. You usually use a delay that's a bit larger than the human reaction time at the very least, to give the player room to act.

5.   Don't just copy- stand out

While making "Darker Souls: The Adventures of Hard Game 3" might seem appealing at first, but you'll soon notice that it isn't quite selling as well as you might want it to.

This is because the gaming industry is constantly craving innovation. Gamers aren't just looking for another version of a game they've already played. They're looking for a similar, but an innovative experience.

6. Don't bite off more than you can chew

This comes back to our past point about a 3D MMORPG. If you're developing a game for yourself, then you need to ensure that it is a feat you can actually accomplish. Now, I don't want to be a party popper and tell you that you *can't* do something.

On the other hand, you should be realistic with yourself. How much time are you planning to dedicate to the game? How large is the team? How experienced are all of you?

All of these factors impact heavily on how well you can do as a game developer. If you've got a small team that plans to work for 2-3 hours a day that are just starting out- don't start with a complex, 100-hour playtime RPG. Instead, you might just want to start with a heavily stylized platformer.

7. Don't fall into the more mechanics trap

When we think of games that have stood the test of time, we rarely think of hyper-complex JRPGS. More often, we will think of titles such as Sonic or Super Mario Bros.

These games don't have too many mechanics going for them. Heck, in Super Mario Bros you can basically just run, jump, and shoot (on occasion) and yet, it is one of the biggest classics of our time, with additional games coming out every year.

Just because your game could have more mechanics doesn't mean it should. Getting the core gameplay right is much more important than adding some obscure peripheral mechanic.

Mechanic bloat is a real thing, and your players might feel awkward playing a game with too many mechanics to consider. Not only may this make the game needlessly hard, but it might also make it borderline unplayable.

8.   Pay attention to the little things

One of the most successful indie game studios of our time is SuperGiant games, with games such as Banner Saga, Hades: Battle Out of Hell, and Transistor getting mind-blowing reviews on most platforms.

So, what can you learn from this studio? Are they simply master storytellers? Do they have the best art that has ever graced the world? Maybe they've just cracked some secret code for satisfying gameplay?

While all of these are partly there, the biggest thing they do is pay attention to minute details. For example, in Hades: Battle Out of Hell, there are hundreds of fully voiced lines for every character. A detail that later turns out to be plot-relevant is the fact that the main character always has his feet on fire.

Now, they could've just made his feet look red and had that be it. Instead, he leaves different footprints based on the environment he's stepping on.

This is not a necessary detail; however, those small things make you appreciate the game world so much more.

9.   Accept criticism

Your first game sucks. I know it's hard to hear, and I know you've probably got dozens of ideas for revolutionary mechanics, but it simply sucks.

My first game sucked as well; even my own brother didn't have the heart to pretend to like it. And you know what? That's perfectly okay. You don't need to make a perfect first project in order to learn from it.

What's more, you will get ideas from it, ideas on how you could've done certain things better. By applying these ideas, you will grow as a game developer.

When I say you should accept criticism, I don't just mean of the "this game sucks" variety. I mean that you should take the opinions of your players seriously; after all, they might not know why something feels bad, but they will sure as hell feel that it does.

Similarly, if players like something, do more of it! Having more of a good thing is rarely bad, and many games go through a whole cycle of re-development.

10. Get Playtesters

It can be easy to fall into the trap that you don't need anyone playtesting your game. After all, you'd know if it wasn't fun, right? Wrong.

You're the person that has sunk in dozens of hours into learning how to make games, only to sink in dozens more into actually making them. This doesn't make for the most impartial of observers. Ideally, you will love playing your game, but there is every chance that you won't. After all, after a certain point it is simply a job.

Now, I'm not saying you will never enjoy playing your game, but there will certainly be days where you'll be unable to look at it.

Because of this, you'll want playtesters. These are people that will play the game and give you their unique and objective opinion on it. Okay, for early testing, you might want to use acquaintances, friends, and family. Keep in mind that they are not always objective; however, they'll do if you've got no other alternative.

I also suggest finding people to play it on the internet. People on the internet are always willing to scrutinize someone's lifelong efforts.

11. Try out different approaches

The good thing about developing games independently is that you don't have a tight deadline. You can try out anything you think is fun and lose nothing over it.

Trying out a variety of different things is one of the biggest advantages of developing a game as a side hustle. If you find that something works very well, you can do more of it, or if you find that something doesn't work well, you can ditch it.

Chapter Six

The Basics of RPG Maker And Creating An RPG

RPG Maker is a game engine that was designed to help you create 2D RPGs. The RPG Maker VX Ace edition is what we'll be using for this tutorial. It is one of the simplest kinds of RPG Maker, and it uses Ruby to boot.

The idea behind this chapter is to get you acquainted with RPG Maker and introduce some of the things you can do in it by using your Ruby knowledge. While sure, you can learn RPG Maker by yourself, there's a variety of pitfalls and errors that, while easily avoided by someone experienced, are easy for a beginner to fall into.

In case you decide against using RPG Maker in order to create a game, you'll still find the latter portion of this chapter useful, as I will be dissecting what it means to be an RPG, as well as how to design one properly.

In this chapter, we'll go over enough material for you to create a basic 2D RPG. Keep in mind everything you've learned from the MUD, though.

Taking A Look At It

First, let's take a look at the essential structure of the RPG Maker program, as well as how each part of it interacts with the rest of them.

The lowest-level structure that the engine will let you access is the RGSS3, also known as the Ruby Game Scripting System. It is based on Ruby with some slight modifications and governs all the game's components. This ranges from the way battles are run, how maps are generated, and how things on the screen move.

Now, it's notable that when developing in RPG Marker, you won't even have to edit the scripts themselves a lot of the time.

As for the RPG Maker platform's basic functions, I'll trust that you'll learn those by yourself in case you decide to use it for your game development.

The Pros And Cons

Like any other method of game development, using RPG Maker has its own pros and cons. In this section, we'll be going over them in order to determine whether it has what you're looking for in creating your game.

Pros

- It provides you with a basic outline from which you can start working on your game. It comes with all the basic concepts necessary to create a game such as looping, delta time, input, and windows.

- It is jam-packed with pre-made assets for you to use. It even has pre-made characters, weapons, and other entries. This gives you a template that can kick start some of the creative processes of making your game.

- It's easy to script in it. After all, if you already know Ruby, then you're almost ready to start scripting with it. The commands are also fairly simple, so you'll get to grips with it quickly.

- It's easy to use and will get you to your first RPG quickly. You could go from zero to a fully fledged RPG within as little as a year.

Cons

- There's little chance for you to make money. Short of a game like To the Moon, you're unlikely to make any cash off of games made in RPG Maker due to the intrinsic stigma that they carry with themselves. This is because many customers are wary of RPG Maker games due to the ease of game creation.

- You're essentially forced into a turn-based battle system. You won't be working with a Diablo-like strategy or anything similar. It's early Final Fantasy or bust.

- All the tiles and characters have constant tile sizes, meaning that you will have a bit less artistic customization.

- You'll find it easier to go into a different engine at a certain point than to keep using RPG Maker. This applies especially to more advanced games.

So, essentially, RPG Maker is great for a hobbyist project. Alternatively, it's great if you're simply looking to learn how to develop a fully fledged RPG. On the other hand, if you intend to create a complex, commercial RPG, then RPG Maker probably isn't the system you want to be using.

Now, if that's all good with you, let's get into some beginner scripting.

Scripting In RPG Maker

Before you start scripting, you should back up your game. After all, if you mess something up with your tinkering, you'll want to be able to put it back the way it was. Unfortunately, RPG Maker does not highlight syntax errors, and one or two of those in the wrong place could render the game unplayable until you look at it again.

Another tip I have is to write everything in a separate file. If you're creating a new monster, I'd write it in another file, then test it by itself until it works. I would only copy and paste it into RPG Maker afterward, so it's less likely for you to make a syntax error.

You'll need to understand 3 basic components of how you can introduce new things to the RPG you're making.

These are the addition and modification of existing classes. The Gosu tutorial prepared you quite well for this, as almost everything in the RPG Maker engine is both shown as classes and run as classes.

You can create new classes to add brand new functions and windows to the game logic within. Alternatively, we can modify the classes already there to alter the flow of in-game portions.

You can also switch the events in the engine through the use of methods. The Ruby methods you're used to are helpful in that they will let you put your thoughts to paper when defining what is within the game.

This can sometimes speed up the development process because you aren't working too much with the visual interface, which is quite a lot clunkier than simply writing scripts. With that being said, there are also times when the visual interface is faster, so use your time wisely.

Finally, there are switches and variables. Regardless of whether you're altering classes or calling brand new methods, you'll require a way to generate data from those changes. Usually, this is done by setting switches or by setting up variables.

Usually, we will use these when we code behavior for NPCs. This applies twice over for enemies such as high-tier bosses, which dynamically react to the party's decisions.

In case all you're tinkering with is the visuals and the user interface, all you'll need to know is to modify the classes that are already there. Maybe you'll add an additional command to a window that's already there? If you do that, then RPG Maker will run that code whenever it encounters that function.

In case you're taking it a step further and have decided to use code in order to do in-game logic, in that case you'll want to write out brand new methods which are set off in Events and you might want to set Switches to alter some of the game's most core functions.

If you're just altering the game's basic visuals, then I would suggest you stick to fiddling with the classes already in place. As an example of this, you could add an additional aspect to a window that's already there.

Classes

Almost all the functions of RPG Maker are actually chunks of Ruby code. It goes without saying that there are absolutely tons of this code. Thankfully, it's rather well organized.

There are five essential groups of classes:

1. **Game Objects** - The Game objects, often referred to as GOs, are the game's fundamental building blocks. They will determine all stats, as well as all the mechanics you put into the RPG. They also have a role in the aesthetic of the game.

2. **The RPG Sprites** - The sprites are the essential component of graphics and are the fundamental building block of your game's aesthetic.

3. **The Module** - These are there in order to figure out what the global variables are within the RPG in addition to how you can interact with the game's world.

4. **Windows** - This class group defines all the game's menus and text display methods.

5. **Scenes** - This class group is used to determine game phases as well as screens (e.g. the menu screen, combat screen, and others.)

Let me give you an example. Classes in RPG Maker are titled in the following format: (WhatKindOfObject)_(WhatItDoes)

Due to this, the engine classes tend to be quite easy to get to grips with. The Game_Actor game object is used in order to establish the game object it refers to as an actor. These are usually members of the hero's party or the hero themselves. This goes further to other classes that will help you understand what they do through their nomenclature.

Window_BattleStatus is used to define the window in which the party's status is shown...in battle.

When you get used to this, you'll find that it makes it extremely easy to alter just the parts you want to change up.

The Different Forms Of Data

If there's a part of RPG Maker that you want to change, then chances are you'll be able to do that through the Ruby programming language. This can also be done in real-time, letting you monitor the game's state at any point in its compilation.

The first thing that we'll be looking at as an example is a simple enemy feature design. The enemy should be able to tell when our character uses a spell we'll call "Shielding." when it notices that the player has used that, then it will use its "Piercing Strike" ability like so:

1. Enter the "Database" section. From there, navigate to Troops, and write down that it should happen at the turn's end.

2. In this event, we'll call a Ruby method, checking every party member. We do this through RPG Maker's special syntax and traditional Ruby code.

3. If we detect one of our party members to have the state ID corresponding to Shield (that is character.state?(17) is true) then we can make a switch.

4. Now, navigate back to the Database folder and go into enemies. Here we need to give the enemy the ability we plan for it to use. It's important to attach to this the condition that the player has used Shielding beforehand.

Using Variables and Conditions

If you're looking for a bit more direct of a way to interact with your code, then you'll find it in set variables and conditional branch event actions. These can not only call a method, but can also use its result immediately.

So, let's say that you want to check if anyone in your party has the Holy Attack skill (perhaps because you want to give it as loot for defeating a boss?) We can do this by adding a conditional branch that will then call the Ruby method to look through our characters' skills. In case they do have Holy Attack, the outcome will be "true" and if they don't have the skill, then it will output false.

Now, you might be thinking "but we could also do this with switches!" While that is true, you could also do it by just hard-coding it in binary, but Ruby does it quicker.

Any event in RPG Maker has an all-purpose "Script" action. This is capable of running any free-form Ruby code, as long as it is properly written. This differs from set variables and conditional branches because it simply doesn't return any data back to the initial event.

This is the easiest way you can set off multiple switches/variables. Alternatively, you can use script actions to execute things that are quicker to write manually than they are to access through the point and click interface.

User Interface and Saving

As we've already considered, the windows you see within the game are found somewhere in the code. Sure, you won't find all the graphics code on it. However, you'll find everything that defines the window and its behavior.

In case you're fond of adding additional manus, and adding or removing visuals, then the chances are that you want to change a Scene or Window class. In these cases, you'll be able to modify the commands that are on the screen, and not only that, you'll also be able to change what the commands do.

Now, a crucial aspect of the savegames in RPG Maker is that they are unable to save the state of your Ruby world. For example, if you made a new variable tracking how many apples a player has collected. Let's say they collect 10 before saving and exiting; when they go back in, they'll find that they have 0.

In order to fix this, you have to ensure that everything you need to persist between saves is found within $game_switches or variables that are saved the right way.

Now, all of this is still quite bare bones, however, it gives you a foundation to go off of.

If you'd like to pursue RPG Maker more seriously, then I suggest checking out their tutorials, as well as practicing a lot. With programming, the more practice you get, the more you'll improve.

Chapter Seven

Genre-Specific Tips

In this chapter, we'll be leaving aside the generic game design advice from before. While there are some things that we can apply to essentially any game, there are also extremely genre-specific things.

In this chapter, I'll be going through some of the most popular game genres on Steam and giving you pointers on how to create games in that genre. These pointers will range from programming concepts you'll want to learn to game design aspects you'll want to focus on.

So, without further ado, let us begin:

Roguelite/Roguelike

A roguelike is a procedurally generated game relying on replay value. Every playthrough should be different, and they are generally made so that you can get through them in one sitting. A lack of permanent progression also characterizes them.

Roguelites, however, are significantly more popular, despite the fact these are often combined into one category. A roguelite, much like a roguelike, relies on replay value and a procedurally generated game world. However, unlike a roguelike, roguelites use some sort of permanent progression system in between runs.

This can range from permanent upgrades to your character, like for example, Hades: Battle Out of Hell to simply unlocking different items and characters, such as in The Binding of Isaac.

A good thing about roguelikes/roguelites is that they are able to create playtimes of upwards of 100 hours with significantly less content than most other game genres.

So, what knowledge do you need to pay special heed to when developing a roguelike?

The Programming Side

The first thing that you'll need to pay a lot of attention to is the procedural generation aspect. If the algorithm isn't up to par, then you'll exhaust the number of room combinations fairly quickly.

Once your players have seen every room a couple of times, the game starts getting more stale. In order to prevent this, you have to ensure that you're using the best procedural generation that you can.

Next, we'll consider balance. The whole thing about roguelikes is that you'll lose a lot of your first playthroughs. Because of this, you should make a relatively steep learning curve to the game. Don't be afraid if it takes you, the developer, days to get to the final boss.

With that being said, it's alright to leave some unbalanced combinations that leave the player feeling extremely powerful. For example, The Binding of Isaac has multiple item combinations that practically win the run on the spot, and it's one of the most popular roguelikes ever despite that.

The next thing you'll want to ensure your game has is post-run content. Just because a player finished the game once doesn't mean that you have to put a game over screen and call it a day.

Instead, make it so that you need to beat the first "final boss" multiple times in order to unlock a new one. Or maybe add higher difficulty settings and challenges for the die-hard players.

Furthermore, the first thing you'll want to worry about in a roguelike is the backend. You don't need to think about the user interface or graphics at first. Simply using placeholder graphics (or even plain text) is perfectly fine.

You'll also want to separate your user's interface to the backend. Rather than keeping the two tied together, you'll want to split them so that you can work on one without disturbing the other.

Make sure that you get saving out of the way quickly. You don't want to be far into creating the game or even almost finished before looking at the savegames titan.

If you're building a pure roguelike, rather than a roguelite, then you may skip this, as you won't need any savegames.

Next, ensure that you design a debug environment early on. Instead of going around the game world in search of bugs while relying on randomness to give you the items you need, make it so that you can spawn things in as you go along.

Finally, make sure that you don't go into optimization immediately. A lot of newbie developers delve into optimizing their game far before it is finished. The only things you need to debug at first are actual errors. There's time to optimize the game's performance after you're done making it.

That's it for the sheer programming prowess side of things. Now, let's get into the design elements that are integral in making a successful roguelite.

Design

Now then, what are the biggest design elements that you need to ensure you're respecting when creating a roguelike?

1. No One Hits

This is one I can't stress enough. There are few things more frustrating for a player than making one minor misstep and winding up dead.

Sure, it might sound cool to give an epic monster an attack that just straight up kills anything in its path. While this is an idea that sounds cool in theory, it's a horrible game design idea in practice.

For example, in Nethack, the Medusa used to be a random spawn that would pop up in a random room within the game's deeper dungeons.

Simply seeing Medusa was enough to kill you...so you can bet that prompted many rage quits.

Today, newer versions of Nethack put medusa on her own special floor where players can be prepared for her. Alternatively, some developers choose not to put her in at all.

2. *Have Some Secret Items*

While it can be fun to play a roguelike where you already know all the items you're getting, roguelikes put a lot of accent on that crucial aspect of randomness. If it is not respected, then the game might lose its roguelike 'feel.'

Instead of just having items spawning randomly, it's often a good idea to put in a loot box or random item that will give you one of a varied assortment of items.

If you're making a game such as Nethack, then it is a design staple to include difficult to identify items. Such as the potions of See Invisible and Fruit Juice having the same pop-ups after you use them.

3. *Powerup Synergy Is Good*

There's nothing so dissatisfying out there than finding a cool, unique combination of items in a game... only to find out that they don't stack.

The powerups within your game should flow into one another. Rather than stepping on each other's toes, I suggest making separate lists of powerups that work together.

Now, I'm not saying there shouldn't be some powerups that work badly together. That is an absolutely crucial element of roguelike design as well. However, instead of having all of your powerups be along the lines of "+10% ATK" make it so that, say, there's one item called Knife, giving you 10 attacks.

Then you can make an item called the sword of knives, and have it double the effectiveness of all the knives in the player inventory, at the cost of 30 defense.

Having that kind of tradeoff between offense and defense also puts the item in a specific niche. A player won't take it if they're going for a defensive or "tanky" build.

4. Minimize In-Run Grind

During any given run, you want the player to be playing for keeps. You want to limit the number of avenues through which they can grind out an advantage.

This is especially relevant if you're making a roguelike/roguelite that isn't based upon a finite number of rooms finalized by a final boss. For example, Rogue itself has a food timer, where food will only pop up once the game generates a new level. This means that players need to be very careful about how much time they spend grinding.

5. Pick A Road

There are 2 main "kinds" of roguelike/lite that you can make. The first is a roguelike that's much like... well... Rogue. There, there's a large focus on randomness and using one-use items and attrition in general.

There, your character starts relatively strong, and the enemies get stronger at a faster pace so that you are forced to use the limited use items.

On the other hand, you have roguelikes like The Binding of Isaac where both you and the enemies get progressively stronger. You are meant to know what the items do, and there's far less randomness.

6. Give the Player Some Consistency

Most roguelikes these days (other than those made by Nethack purists and the like) are made with a variety of powerups and "builds" you can make. Doing this with a completely random distribution of these buffs is nigh-impossible.

Because of this, games have incorporated ways that help you increase the likelihood of getting that synergistic item or powerup. Hades: Battle Out of Hell has the God's keepsakes and the black mirror, while Isaac has the reroll machine and the active dice items.

This type of pseudo-consistency lets your player gamble on high-risk builds and feel like they've still got some control over what's happening.

7. Enemy Variety

It's not enough to simply make varied maps to have a good roguelike. You also need to make varied enemy designs. By this I don't just mean enemies that look different. They need to move differently, attack differently, and feel different.

Enemy variety is possibly even more important than environment variety. This is because while the environment is largely in the back of the player's mind, as merely a background element, enemies are at the forefront.

You want the player to feel stumped, to feel challenged whenever they encounter a brand new enemy. In order to facilitate this feeling, you should try to put in as many varied attacks, movesets, and designs as you can into your roguelike.

8. Don't Feature Bloat

A lot of more modern roguelikes have what I like to call "feature bloat." When you open your character screen, you see 200 different numbers, usually without any explanation as to what they do.

While having a steep learning curve is fine, most players that see this will simply walk away. An easier approach to take is to introduce new mechanics and stats slowly as the player progresses through the game.

Hades: Battle Out of Hell does this excellently. At first, it only presents you with choices of up to 3 abilities to pick from on each powerup room.

Soon enough, you're choosing from 4 weapon aspects of each of the 8 weapons, as well as a keepsake, pondering about heat, and picking up a legendary keepsake before you even start your run!

This way, your new players aren't overwhelmed, but you still leave some material to keep the veterans engaged.

9. *Achievements And Difficulty*

Speaking of veterans. With gaming becoming more and more popular these days, there are a lot more "hardcore" gamers than before. These are the people putting on 200, or sometimes over 2000 hours into a game.

You want to capture this playerbase. Not only will they buy your game, fund it on Kickstarter, and buy your merch, they will make online content that popularizes your game.

To keep these people entertained, you should incorporate a variety of different achievements and difficulty levels into your game. For example, The Binding of Isaac: Afterbirth has a character that can take a total of 2 hits in a room at most.

With ideal items, they may be able to tank through 3 hits. Completing the game on the hardest difficulty with this character unlocks you a special achievement. This is precisely the kind of thing you want to keep in your game.

10. Don't Shy Away From Uniqueness

The field of roguelikes and roguelites is vast and saturated. Countless games are competing for your player's attention all at once. If you are to shy away from making your game stand out, you'll get none of them.

Furthermore, this genre is one of the best when it comes to taking bold risks, as a single game that succeeds at a niche can spawn a whole genre. For example, Slay The Spire made the whole (now massive) genre of turn-based deck building roguelikes.

Taking a risk on tackling a new theme or design is a great idea when developing a roguelike. If you want another example of it paying out, look at Risk of Rain 2. They changed from a side-scrolling 2D platformer to a 3D bullet hell roguelike with some platforming elements, and suddenly they're on the best-selling page on Steam.

Turn-Based RPG

The most popular genre of game by far, the Role Playing Game is a staple of the gaming industry like no other. In fact, it is so difficult to define what exactly *is* an RPG that I decided to split it up into two distinct categories, one dealing with turn-based RPGs and the other dealing with real-time or action RPGs.

The Programming Side

So, what are the most important things for you to know when it comes to programming a turn-based RPG?

The first is how to streamline classes properly. You don't need to be making a brand new class every time you want to create another kind of player character. Instead, it's usually a good idea to make a single class for all player characters, and another for all enemies.

Some games take this a step further and simply have one class both for enemies and players. Let's look at Darkest Dungeon for an idea as to why this works so well.

Darkest Dungeon equips every character with 4 distinct moves that can deal either damage or stress. If a heroes' stress gauge hits 200, they suffer a heart attack, putting them at 0 health. However, enemies don't have a stress gauge.

So, how can you create this while using only one class for all the parameters? Simple, you create a class for all the characters, that includes both stress and health. You just don't display it (or have it affect) monsters.

You do the same for attacks; the heroes' attack can just have a stress value of 0 due to the fact monsters can't suffer stress damage.

You will also need to learn how to comment and annotate your code properly. It isn't enough to just be able to *write* a turn-based RPG. You also need to be able to work on it properly.

If you don't properly comment your code, you'll find yourself going back and realizing you simply don't know what some elements of your own code even are.

This is not the best position to be in. This makes debugging a much, much harder process than it has to be.

Furthermore, if you want to bring someone on your team to help you out with programming, they'll have a much more difficult time helping you code if they don't know what each portion of the code is even for.

Truthfully, coding a turn-based RPG isn't too difficult by itself. The difficulty mostly comes from handling graphics and different mechanics found within the game.

The Design Side

On the design side of things... there's a lot to say. The genre of turn-based RPGs is probably the vastest genre of games out there, meaning that there are a lot of things that you can get right... and a lot of things you can get wrong.

1. Perfectly Balanced, As All Things Should Be

The lack of balance in many turn-based RPGs stems from multiple factors. The first is simply that the "class" the game dev likes the most is the most likely to outclass the rest of the classes.

Now, even if you don't use classes or party compositions, you still need to pay attention to skill balance. You don't want any skills to feel useless. You also don't want any of them to feel completely overpowered.

Finding this middle ground can be rather difficult. For this reason, I suggest having a separate minigame where you can simulate multiple player classes/builds fighting.

This lets you pit the things that seem over-tuned or under-tuned one against the other in order to determine if it really is like that.

Now, that isn't the only way an RPG can be imbalanced. If monsters are getting stomped, even though the player is just bashing "attack" then that's also a balance issue.

2. *Following The Basic 4 Virtues*

It's a fairly popular belief that there is a set of basic principles under which any turn-based RPG should be designed. The 4 virtues that any RPG should follow are:

- Emergent Complexity: The complexity of the game doesn't come from having a thousand things going on. Rather, it comes out of ten things intertwining and interacting in subtle ways. Keep the rules simple, but ensure that they can facilitate more complex mechanics.

- Clarity: The player shouldn't have to wonder, "what could I have done better?" Instead, their tactical successes and failures alike should be intrinsically obvious to the player.

- Determinism: Your game should be sufficiently deterministic that a player playing skillfully and using proper tactics will almost always wind up with a victory.

- Randomness: There should be some randomness in the system to facilitate a player being able to feel lucky. However, the luck given in the system should never be able to trump skillful play.

A great example of all four of these is The Darkest Dungeon. It has a handful of in-combat mechanics. However, these mechanics interact in ways that can even create a complex PvP meta.

Every decision is meaningful, where you'll place a hero which skills you'll equip, what trinkets you'll put on them, etc.

Your mistakes and victories also tend to be obvious; the in-game narrator tends to point out mistakes and bad decisions. For example, pursuing great rewards by turning off the light mid-dungeon, even though you know low-light conditions make stress damage more potent.

It has enough determinism that a skilled player will almost always be able to clear the game. There are countless speedruns out there, as well as challenge runs such as "no light" and similar. This is the hallmark of a well-designed game.

Despite all of this, it still has a small RNG element in its crit, miss, virtue, and flaw systems. All of these are mostly based on luck (you can influence the probabilities, but they are still random) however, they don't get into the way of strategic gameplay.

3. Specialization

As a rule of thumb, a generalist character should always be worse than a specialized one in their expertise area. The optimal composition for a character should be mostly specialized skills.

This is because having characters (or even skills) excel in one area while lacking in others brings tactical depth. This helps give you enough design space to facilitate a lot of different kinds of characters.

If you don't do this, and rather opt for a variety of generalists, you'll wind up with something much akin to playing chess with just queens. Sure, it might sound fun at first, but you'll soon understand there's little to no tactical depth to it.

This doesn't just apply to friendly characters. Enemies should also be specialized most of the time. It's okay to let a boss do multiple things well; however, regular enemies should be good at one or two things. This lets the player have options on how to counter those specific enemies, further increasing the game's tactical depth.

4. Different Difficulty Settings

Turn-Based RPGs are the genre of game that suffers most from not having proper difficulty levels. Due to being rooted in strategy, if your game doesn't have different difficulty levels, that's like playing a chess bot without one.

If you're better than it, then you'll just stomp. If you're worse than it, you'll just get frustrated and quit. The same applies to video games.

For example, most of the negative reviews on Darkest Dungeon's Steam page come from the time when the game didn't have its Radiant difficulty, meant to make the game easier for beginner players.

5. Don't Forget The Story

Just because most people enjoy the combat aspect of turn-based RPGs the most doesn't mean you should slack off on the story. A game needs to be a comprehensive art form.

You might want to step away from the combat every now and again and recap the story so far. Think about how the encounters make sense within the story, as well as how it should progress past that point.

6. Fast Travel

This is a bigger deal with action RPGs; however, as Final Fantasy shows us, sometimes this design mistake makes its way into turn-based games. This is especially true for some JRPGs, which for some reason just outright refuse to incorporate fast travel in the game.

Now, I get it; you want your players to explore the intricate world you've created. That's cool. Nobody is telling you not to let them do that. However, keep in mind that some players simply don't care that much about the world and the environments.

Sure, maybe that moving stone monument of the city founder took you days to get working, but Joe wants to get past it in a few seconds.

This is why all games should have fast travel, at the very least between already explored zones. Secondarily, it lets players get from A to B quicker, letting them progress the story.

7. Non-Linear Level Ups

A good feature to have in any RPG. I'm rather tired of every other RPG just having me get XP and then leveling me up and letting me put a point or two in one or two stats. Instead of this, players love it when you let them customize!

A good example of this is the grid from Final Fantasy X. It lets you follow a path when you want and take a completely nonlinear route when you don't. This is also present in Path of Exile and is one of the game's biggest draws.

8. Pick Your Audience Carefully

While this applies to any kind of game, it's extremely important for turn-based RPGs to decide what audience you want to target. Sure, by including different difficulty modes you can get players from all kinds of backgrounds, but your main audience will remain the same.

I've found that gamers fall into four broad categories:

The Casual: The casual gamer doesn't care that much about intense detail and is more fond of getting stronger than they are of being challenged. If there's a fight that takes them 5-10 tries, they'll likely not come back to the game again. If you're targeting this audience, try to focus more on the game mechanics' entertainment value, rather than their balance.

The Hardcore: These folks want their challenges and they want it now. They are much less interested in the progression than they are in the intrinsic challenge of your game. Sure, they might like the story, but they still want their fights to be like the hardest Dark Soul's boss.

The Mathematician: These gamers want to be crunching numbers all day long. They want to be able to draw up graphs and theorycraft their build so they can fully optimize their character. They aren't so much in it for the challenge, as they like big numbers popping up on their screen. They aren't averse to grinding XP to help themselves improve.

The Bookworm: These people want to read your game like a book. The gameplay is a narrative device to them, rather than something they partake in for its own sake. They want to experience the story and carefully crafted world of your game.

Naturally, almost nobody falls completely into one of these; however, there's usually a dominant one in any gamer. Your game should ideally be targeting one of these.

With that being said, you shouldn't ignore the rest; it's ideal to create mechanics that will facilitate every kind of play.

For example, Hades: Battle Out of Hell does this by having an easy mode for the casual gamers, a HEAT system that makes everything harder for hardcore gamers (the highest HEAT setting hasn't been beaten with every weapon yet.) It has a variety of builds for the mathematician to think about, and a deep story told through beautiful art for the bookworm.

9. No Mandatory Grinds

There's little point in forcing the player to grind out common mobs in a single-player game. This is one of the biggest complaints that people often have about the genre - its repetitiveness. While the repetitive nature isn't intrinsic, a lot of game developers think that just because a game is a turn-based RPG, you should have to spend 10 hours grinding up your stats to beat the final boss.

Now, I'm not saying grinding shouldn't be an option, or that it shouldn't be useful. I'm saying you shouldn't have to grind for the main story progression. If you want to beat the secret boss, get all achievements, or something similar, then grinding is appropriate.

10. Make Sure The Visuals Have Oomph

Now, this is a bit of a weird one. Even though turn-based RPGs are hailed as one of the genres with the least regard for graphics, smooth animations and a clear visual direction push it further than most.

Due to the turn-based nature of it, you aren't able to generate dynamics the same way an action RPG does. Instead, most good turn-based RPGs do this by incorporating quality, high-impact animations into the game.

Let's take a look at Darkest Dungeon again, look at any of its attack animations. Each of them ends at the peak of a swing, even though they are only a few frames long, they add dynamics to the combat and make it feel more real.

11. Plan It From A To Z

Turn-based RPGs are the hardest type of game to execute well without a well-designed plan. If you don't have a plan from the start, you could find yourself backtracking not just on your code but also on story elements, maybe even gameplay mechanics.

These types of issues are what lead to games being stuck in development hell for years on end. In order to avoid this issue, try to plot out your whole game in one breath.

Real-Time RPGs

Real-time RPGs (also known as action RPGs) are the second subset of the role-playing game we'll be taking a close look at. Some turn-based RPG design elements still stay here, so we will not be repeating them.

The Programming Side

Depending on the type of game you're making, you might be looking at the most intelligence-tasking time of your life here.

There's a variety of different real-time RPGs, so it's hard to say what *exactly* you'll need to learn; however, there are some general things almost every action RPG relies on.

The first is collisions. Now, in your head, it might seem simple to realize when a hammer has hit a rock. For the game it is much less so. In fact, collision detection is usually the part that bugs up the worst.

Unfortunately, it's absolutely critical for any kind of real-time RPG. Because of this, I advise you to use an engine such as Unity to handle it for you, as coding collisions from scratch can be rather difficult.

If you're so inclined, you might decide that you want a 3D game. In this case, there's a whole can of worms. Not only will you need to learn 3D based collisions, but you'll also need to get to grips with coding 3D game physics and vectors.

All in all, action RPGs are the hardest kind of game to code from scratch. Luckily, some engines make this much easier for you. Unity, for example, is the most popular game engine for action RPGs among beginners (more on that in the next chapter.)

You'll also need to learn how to use tilesets properly and create more intricate maps, not only graphically but also how to program them to not have your game fall apart.

If you're really dead-set on hard-coding it, then I suggest you make at least 1 prototype of every other kind of game on this list, as an action RPG is a combination of them all in a way. Plus, maybe it'll get you off the crazy idea of making a 3D RPG alone.

The Design Side

A lot of the design tips from the turn-based RPG apply here, so I won't be listing those again. Instead, I'll be focusing on those aspects that are unique to action RPGs.

1. Pay Attention To Level Design And Map Variety

Much like the roguelike, an action RPG needs to pay careful attention to how the levels are designed, as well as how good the maps are.

Even if you're creating an open-world RPG, consider every area as its own separate level. You need to make it so that the player isn't bored by constantly exploring into nothing, but at the same time you want to give them the feeling of a vast world.

Map variety is also very important. Action RPGs are generally designed with long playtimes in mind, meaning that the player will be looking at your maps for around 40 to 60 hours. If the maps are dull, that'll greatly affect their enjoyment of the game.

2. Focus On Worldbuilding

In a real-time RPG, the player will spend a lot of time looking at and engaging with your world. If you have a world that is set in 2099 Russia, but the society works and has the morals of modern Western society, that breaks the immersion.

Since real-time RPGs are much more focused on immersion than other kinds of games, you want to avoid this at all costs. Pay attention to your world and try to make sure it makes as much sense as possible in all respects.

3. Avoid Repetitive Gameplay Patterns

This is a sneaky killer of many games and is the reason why Assassin's Creed Unity flopped. Each combat encounter felt and played the same. Sure, maybe the enemies looked different, but you were doing the same thing.

You want to avoid this. The easiest way to avoid it is by including a variety of different weapons that each have their own sets of abilities. Alternatively, you could include a variety of abilities that do different things.

A combo system is also useful for this. You can have a variety of different combos that have different follow-up events that happen to the enemy when they are hit.

This isn't only relevant for the player, but also for the enemies. Part of the reason why Dark Soul's bosses are so great is that they don't have simple patterns. Each of them has 4-5 attacks by themselves. Even some of the regular enemies have 3 or more.

If your game has boars, whose only attack is rushing straight at you, that will get old fast. If you must keep the boring boars, then I suggest creating more enemies with more attacks.

Having a lot of enemies, even if they don't have too many attacks, can also give the illusion of variety and have your player be engaged for longer.

4. Post-Game Content

Just because you finished the game's main plot doesn't mean you should be forced to stop playing or start a new game. Adding optional late-game bosses is a great way to further the playtime of a game.

If you want a game that finalizes once you finish the main story, then it's a good idea to add a New Game+, making the game harder. Rather than simply scaling the numbers up for enemy damage and health, I suggest giving the enemies unique skills for NG+, as well as altering their spawn points and rates.

You don't need to make too many changes to your game in order to include post-game content, and it can really help your game get and retain players.

Another (relatively) simple way to extend the game is by adding multiplayer. I don't mean a MMORPG obviously. But either instance-based fights or PvP fights between a couple of players.

Platformers

The next category of games will be platformers. Roughly speaking, a platformer is any game that centers around getting from one stage of the map to the next.

The Programming Side

When making a platformer, a lot of the mechanics you'll incorporate will depend on your creative vision. With that being said, it's hard to imagine a platform without jumping, and, well... platforms.

Jumping is actually deceptively complex to program. You need jumping to feel smooth and satisfying; after all, it's what the player will spend most of their time doing.

You will also need to have very precise collision detectors. You wouldn't want the player phasing through the platform and sinking under the map, now would you? That actually happened to me when I was making my first platformer, and trust me; it isn't anywhere near as fun as it sounds.

Past this, you'll need to think hard about the unique mechanics your platformer brings to the table that set it apart from the rest. Whether they be an interesting way to interact with the platforms, or simply a diverse set of powerups.

Furthermore, most platformers will include some kind of enemies. Learning how to make simple AI is extremely important for that.

The Design Side

Creating a platformer is largely on the game designers, rather than the programmers. This is because they're relatively simple to program; however, actually making them enjoyable to play can be extremely challenging.

1. Ensure The UI Is Simple Enough

Your player shouldn't need to navigate through 15 different screens to figure out how to jump. There should be one button to jump, and it should be either W or Space.

If you have any other mechanics, then you should keep them close to the jump button. Having an intuitive and simple interface is very important to any game's success, and even more so, a platformer.

Make sure it's easy to navigate between different menus and settings in the game. If your controls aren't responsive, you've basically failed immediately, as a platformer relies on the player being able to control the fine motions of their character.

2. Everything Important Should Be Visible

You want to make sure that the screen contains all the information the player needs to know at all times. For example, you need to show the player their health. Furthermore, you need to make the platforms different colors/styles from the scenery around it so that they can see where they need to jump (unless that's the level's gimmick, of course.)

If there are any collectibles on screen, the player should be able to see them clearly. And if the player has picked up or equipped any additional powerups, that should be obvious at a glance.

3. Fluid Animations

The movements within a platformer should be smooth and fluid whenever you can make it so.

An "animation state" is a point at which the character is at the moment. What you want are animation states that can go from one to any other one within an instant. Let's say that you are in the middle of the "jump" animation state. If the player now wants to do an attack, they shouldn't need to wait for themselves to land; rather, they should be able to switch from one state to the other immediately.

4. Logical Level Design

Level design is the most crucial component of making a platformer. The level design is what the people playing your games will experience first and foremost. Every single level should be made to be a bit more challenging than the last.

This way, you can constantly keep rewarding your player for learning from the last level. Because of this, you should also try to incorporate parts from past levels into later ones, so the player can feel how much they've improved.

5. A Short Tutorial

If your platformer has a myriad of mechanics, please don't put all of them in the tutorial. When players start playing a platformer, they're expecting themselves to be able to relax while playing.

If your tutorial lasts 15 minutes and is chock-full of tens of different mechanics, then the player will get confused right out of the gate. They may even forget aspects of the game.

Instead, you should make the tutorial short, sweet, and simple. If you want to introduce additional mechanics past that, then you should introduce them with example levels and tutorial sections at the start of levels.

Point-And-Click

Finally, let's look at the simplest kind of game to make. It is a point-and-click game. A point-and-click game is a game where the only mechanic is simply clicking on locations.

Usually, these games are story-focused. However, sometimes you'll find that they include a few mechanical difficulties. For example, rhythm games such as Osu! rely on simple clicking; however, due to the music and rhythm aspect, the game is also mechanically challenging.

The Programming Side

The programming side of making a point-and-click game is mainly focused on detecting input and reacting to it.

In fact, by this point in the book you should be able to make a simple point-and-click game. Make it so that there are two balls, and every time you click on the left ball, a counter goes up, and whenever you click the right one the counter goes down.

When you're done with this, you should understand the fundamental mechanic behind point-and-click games. With that being said, creativity, both in the story and in mechanics, is very easily shown in this kind of game.

For example, the ball example could be used as a mechanic. You could have the left ball be "anger" and the right one to be "calmness." Then, the game could be about presenting the player situations and figuring out how much of a mix of anger and calmness should be used there.

Alternatively, you could make a bog-standard point-and-click adventure game, where pressing on things makes it so that the character interacts with the object. A good example of this is The Henry Stickman series.

Another programming challenge you could face is found within the animations. Sometimes you will need to program how different animations interact and how they trigger based on past decisions.

The Design Side

1. Make Sure All Items Have Their Use

The player will have a lot of items in their inventory (if you're making an adventure/puzzle game.) Make sure that every item your player can pick up is useful.

If you're planning a harder game, you might make the items they find early useful later in the game. On the other hand, if you aren't planning a game that's too difficult, try to make it so that the player is able to use the items they find fairly soon.

2. Try To Get Creative With Items

The simplest items out there, such as water or a bucket, simply aren't interesting. In an adventure game, you can do everything essentially, then don't get stuck on items like these. If you're using an item that you can easily find in real life, you can probably get a more creative item.

So, what's better to use than water or a simple bucket? Exotic vinegar is better than water, and something that's more fun than a bucket is a hollowed-out eagle carcass.

The puzzle would then make you use exotic vinegar with a hallowed out eagle on a fire. Sure, it's still as simple as filling out the carcass with vinegar then spilling it, but that's much more interesting than pouring out water.

3. Adding Layers To Puzzles

A puzzle with layers is usually infinitely more interesting than a puzzle without them. What I mean by this is a puzzle that needs more steps to solve rather than just being A+B=C.

Now, let's take the previous example. We'll need quite a bit of our exotic vinegar if we want to extinguish a huge fire. So, where do we get it? Well, let's say there's a brewery nearby. However, the brewer doesn't want to make any vinegar right now.

Why doesn't he? He's afraid of a mouse that seems to be staring at him relentlessly. So, we need to rid ourselves of the mouse's presence. We grab some cheese, then use it on the mouse. How do we get cheese?

Well, let's say there's an old milk bottle in 1945; we take our time travel machine, grab it from there, and let it ferment up to the current day. Then we've finally got our cheese. We lure away the mouse and get our vinegar.

Now then, what do we do with the dead eagle's body? We can use a hollowed-out carcass in order to make a makeshift bucket by hollowing it out. Let's say a larger bird is sitting on the perch eating bits of an eagle. We would then use our dead eagle's body to give us our makeshift bucket.

4. Signpost Often

Signposts are sets of images and events that lead your players towards getting the right solution.

For example, in the brewery situation, the player could look at their vinegar bottle and see "made in...3 screens to the left." This kind of meta-signpost could then lead the player to the brewery.

From there on you should signpost most of the important decisions for the player. This way, you avoid the most fundamental issue with adventure puzzle games.

That issue is that frequently, the puzzle solutions aren't what the player will immediately think of. Because of this, a player's enjoyment of a puzzle game will often depend on how well the vision of the programmer and the vision of the player agree.

Signposts avoid this issue by letting the player feel smart when they find the signpost and solve an issue themselves.

5.   Multiple Solutions

What if, instead of extinguishing the fire using the vinegar, the player could also reroute the local river to that location?

Your player wants to feel smart about themselves for finding the solution; however, if that solution is too far removed from where they're coming from, then they won't feel like that. Rather, they'll feel frustrated that their solution won't work in the game.

Though this isn't a dealbreaker for most players, you still want to make it as fun as possible for them.

6.   Focus On The Narrative More

In a point-and-click game, we can't really have gameplay that is all that satisfying. After all, it all boils down to simple clicking. Your gameplay is not going to be the main attraction of your game.

So what is then?

The narrative and artistic choices become increasingly more important when making a point-and-click game. Having a cohesive narrative and interesting art is extremely important for a game like this.

Other Kinds of Games

These naturally aren't all the kinds of games out there. There are also pure puzzle games, strategy games, cooking games, dating sims, etc. However, if we were to cover all of them, then this book would be a lot thicker.

It's notable that the design and programming principles covered so far can be applied to those genres. For example, signposting is extremely important when it comes to puzzle games. Similarly, most of the RPG design elements are useful when making a dating sim.

The action RPG programming elements are similar to the ones you need for cooking games.

I suggest you try to create a prototype of each of these. If you manage to do that well, you'll gain enough knowledge to make pretty much any other kind of game.

Chapter Eight

Entering Unity Development

In this chapter, we'll be leaving Ruby behind temporarily in order to delve into Unity.

Unity is one of the most popular game engines out there. It facilitates solo indie game development better than any other game engine on the market. In this chapter, I'll be teaching you how to make a simple project in it.

Unlike RPG Maker, Unity doesn't suffer the stigma of being a low-effort engine.

What Is Unity

Unity is a video game engine capable of outputting both 2D and 3D work. Furthermore, it serves as a useful framework giving you a system that helps you design games both for desktop and for phones. Unity is also capable of making simulations, apps, etc.

Now, the good thing about Unity is that it combines the ability to interact with everything via code, as well as visually. Another excellent boon of Unity is that it's free. While there is an excellent premium version, it isn't necessary for what we will be doing. There have also been some very impressive games made in the free version.

It also allows you just to drop in pretty much any 3D model or picture, even if it's a picture you've just finished working on in Photoshop. It will also let you piece together different importable assets, as well as write code that helps you interact with the surrounding objects. It also supports a variety of different animation styles and will let you animate as well as any other advanced animation system would.

Unity also supports a variety of platforms. You can switch from working on Windows to working for Android in a manner of minutes. This capability is another reason why it's beloved by game developers around the world.

With that being said, one of the most useful things Unity brings to the table is its asset store. This is one of the most expansive and quality asset marketplaces in the world. Here, you'll be able to find basically anything that you need for your game. Do you need art? Maybe you need quality 3D models? You may even need some animations? The Unity Asset Store has it all.

There are also visual systems for scripting like Behave to be found in Unity. In the same vein, you can get experience with high-end shaders, textures etc. It's also fully scriptable, meaning that there's a variety of third-party applications made for it.

What You Shouldn't Use It For

Now, there are some things that Unity simply isn't good for. Now, while people often push the limits of what Unity can and can't do, there remain some things that simply aren't optimal to do in it. An example of this is the creation of models and assets. While you would be able to bring a bunch of cars into Unity as models and then make them race, you usually wouldn't make the same cars within it.

With that being said, if you insist on doing it in Unity, there's a 3D modeling extension called ProBuilder that allows you to do that. If you are going for 2D, there's also a variety of different ways to get to do that within the Unity interface.

Taking The First Steps

Now, the download and installation of Unity are extremely simple. You double click a few buttons and you're there.

Within Unity, there are 3 languages you can program in. Those are C++, C#, and JavaScript. With that being said, there are ways to use Ruby to do this. For example, you could use a Ruby to JavaScript compiler and be done with it. That does make it harder to debug the code, though.

I advise you learn one of the natively supported languages, though if you'd really like to stick to Ruby that is also fine. Keep in mind that you *will* eventually need to expand your horizons past it, though.

Now that you've downloaded Unity. Open it up and let's begin.

First, you'll want to name and assign a place for your project within the project dialog box. You're able to put anything into your project;

Unity does this through importable packages, though at the moment you don't need to add any of those.

I advise not to check anything in that tab unless you know you need it. This is because these packages can sometimes make the size of the files you're using grow several times in size.

Finally, you'll want to pick whether you want your project to be 2D or 3D. This is one of Unity's newer features, as it didn't have a 2D game tooling system natively in place for quite some time. When you pick 2D, then Unity changes a few things to make it easier for you to make a 2D game.

If you want to find the things that you download from the Unity asset store you'll find them in C: \ Users \ Your_Name \ AppData \ Roaming \ Unity \ Asset Store. This is where everything will show up, and if you want to add it to a project, you can just click twice on any of the files here with your project opened up.

Now then, you'll want to press "Create" in the dialog box that pops up when you start Unity. This makes it so that we make a new project, and the default Unity window will greet you. Don't worry if it seems a bit overwhelming at first; you'll soon get used to it.

What You Should See

These are the things you should see in the default window:

- Project- This contains every file within your project. If you just drag-and-drop files from Explorer into the window, Unity will add them to the currently open project.

- Scene: This represents the scene you've opened.

- Hierarchy: This is a list of every game object within the currently open scene.

- Inspector: This displays all the properties of any object you select.

- Toolbar: The toolbar contains a variety of functions ranging from Advance Frame to something much simpler, like Rotate. The most important thing here is that simply clicking "Play" lets you start playing your game immediately.

- The Console Window: This is a window that can get hidden, but it shows all of your code's output. This will sometimes show important debugging info, so don't forget about it.

It's important to mention that there's a separate tab that will open near the Scene tab. This is the game tab, and it pops up whenever you start playing your game. This provides you with somewhat of a playground for testing. It's a debugger's heaven in essence. You can even make scenes during gameplay here by pausing on a scene and switching back. With that being said, if you make changes during play, then you should copy and paste it. To ensure that you never forget that you're in play mode, I suggest coloring it under Edit | Preferences | Colors | Playmode Tint.

Looking At Scenes

Everything that you find in your game is in a scene. Keep in mind that every component, every fragment and letter of code you've written in there is just a scene. The way Unity sees your whole game is essentially just a complex series of scenes that are strung together through programming.

The easiest way to think about scenes is as levels. Sure, can you have 5 levels in one scene file? You could, but most developers simply make it so that the scene files correspond 1 : 1 to levels in-game.

Your scene files are where you'll find lots of the metadata within your game. This means that every little resource you put in there will have its metadata stored there. In general, it's a great idea to save any scenes you were editing before you leave Unity, so you don't lose a bunch of your carefully crafted code.

Within a scene, you won't be able to see your game if you don't put in a camera, and without adding an Audio Listener to any of your many GameObject-s you won't be able to hear anything. With that being said, the Unity engine will by default provide you with both of these.

Structuring Your Game And Adding In Assets

Unlike most other game creation platforms, Unity doesn't let you simply open a file as a substitute for your project, because your project isn't *just* a file when it's done in Unity. Instead, projects will have a variety of different addons like Assets and Libraries within them.

- The Assets Folder: This folder will contain essentially every file you put into your project. This includes all the art, audio, and scripting files you attach to it. This is generally one of the top-level folders when looking at it through the Unity Editor.

- Library: Your library folder will include the metadata for all of your assets. It's the less flashy younger brother of the assets folder.

- ProjectSettings: This folder does exactly what it says on the tin. It remembers all the changes you make to the settings of your project. Its temp folder is used automatically by Unity for temporary things it needs to store.

While all of these portions are found in the system, it's ideal to avoid changing any of the files alone. Even if you just copy and paste to and from Unity, you will still face issues due to how the engine interprets this. In the event you don't opt to utilize the editor for something that needs to be altered, there's a chance it'll malfunction.

On the other hand, if you're bringing a file into Unity, that generally works just fine.

GameObjects

Now, basically everything in Unity is a GameObject. That little ball you designated as your player? A GameObject. The enemies you put all around chasing them? A GameObject. The very ground they roll over? A GameObject. My grandmother's aunt? A GameObject.

This is the base class for almost everything in the Unity engine. You can see the properties of a GO (as we'll refer to GameObjects from now on) by pressing on it through the Inspector window. Whenever you include a GO, it will be invisible until you give it visual properties.

Every GO has 4 properties. They are the Name, Tag, Layer, and the Transform.

Now, the name is just that, a name for the GO. The tag is like its primary property, and the Transform is its position, the way it is rotated, and its scale. Unity uses X as its horizontal axis, Y as its vertical, and Z as its depth axis.

Game development makes quite a bit of use of vectors, which we'll cover in a later part of this series. For now, all you need to know is that the position and the scale of any GO are Vector3 objects. What this means is that they use 3D vectors in order to determine their position and scale. So, by having 3 different values you can assign an object a unique position.

Components

The way that we make GOs do what we want is by adding different components to them. Basically, everything you could add to a GO is a component. All of these components will also show up whenever you use the Inspector window to look at the object. For example, there's the MeshRender and SpriteRender component which are the biggest determinants of how your object looks.

Adding any audio or lighting effects to your object is also done through components. Even the notorious physics effects and collisions are handled through components in Unity. You can also add a variety of different systems, such as particles and path-finding capabilities through components.

Basically, if GOs were the cells in your body, then components would be all the exciting things those cells do. This is why components are one of the most interesting parts of Unity game development.

Now, let's begin. Make a new GO as a cube. You can do this by simply pressing the create other option and then selecting "Cube." I've taken this cube and named it "Enemy" and then another one, which I appropriately named "Hero."

Making The Enemy Chase

We want to make code that will make the Enemy cube follow the Hero cube. Now, setting aside the debate of cubic morality, how do we do that?

Well, the first way is simply to change the Enemy cube's position in every frame by manipulating its transform. However, an easier way is by simply applying physics to the enemy and letting Unity do it for us.

Now, if we want to do it per frame, then that'll need us to think a bit further than "go forward." So, I'm going to make the Enemy move a tad each frame so that we can have precise control over where and how it moves. Naturally, there are also libraries that will significantly shorten this motion for you, such as the very popular iTween.

I'll start by pressing on the Project window and making a new C# script. It will be titled Enemy-INT. In order to put this script up to an object, all we need to do is drag the file where we have the script to the object, or even to the Hierarchy where the object is. After that, Unity will apply the script to the object without us needing to lift a finger.

Now, this script can be streamlined, like by adding a RigidBody to our enemy; however, I tried to keep it simple here. So, how does the script look like?

```
public class EnemyINT: MonoBehavior
{
// All of this will pop up in the inspector window (at least numerically)
public float Speed = 30;
private Transform _heroTransform;
```

```
private Transform _ myTransform;
// All of this will be referred to when the GO is called up
void Start()
{
// Find a GO that has the textual tag "Hero" assigned to it.
// This is another piece of startup code, meaning that it will fire
off whenever this entity appears.
var player = GameObject.FindGameObjectWithTag("Hero");
if (!hero)
{
Debug.LogError(
    "We couldn't find a Hero! Now then, what's a story without
a hero? Get on it, chop chop!.");
}
else
{
// This will find you a reference so that you can alter its
transform to use it later. Note that every save is managed on a
native code call.
_heroTransform= hero.transform;
}
// This references the transform of the player so that we can
utilize it later
_myTransform = this.transform;
```

```
    }
```

// This will make it so that the script is called every frame now

```
    void Update()

    {
```

// This sets the rate of movement as for how quickly the enemy should move toward the hero. Unity treats one unit as a meter, and the Time.deltaTime function will give you the time that it took to get from one frame to the next. If you're running the game at 60FPS (and for this game, you should be) that's 0.0167.

// So, if we want our enemy to move at 2 times that, it means that it will cover .033 units per frame.

```
        var moveAmount = Speed * Time.deltaTime;
        // This makes it so that it updates its position whenever the
        hero moves.
        _myTransform.position =
        Vector3.MoveTowards(_myTransform.position,
            _heroTransform.position, moveAmount);
    }

    }
```

And that's the basic part of it! You should look through this code in detail, and once you've understood it, I suggest experimenting with it a bit. Now, the good thing is that we can reference any component that we've got shown within the editor through code. We can also put a script to any GO, and use their own Start and Update methods, as well as any others you wind up learning.

So, let's presume that the script which will contain the code above needs to find an EnemyINT class. We can just find that component like this:

```
public class EnemyHP: MonoBehavior
private EnemyINT_enemyINT;
// Use this for initialization.
void Start () {
  // This refers to the EnemyINT script which is found within
  the attached GO.
  var enemyINT= this.GetComponent<EnemyINT>();
}
// The Update method works once per frame.
void Update () {
  _enemyINT.MoveTowardsPlayer();
}
```

Whenever you finish fiddling with your code in MonoDevelop, or whichever editor you use for your code (I use Notepad++) then you go back into Unity, you'll notice that there's a bit of lag. This happens because whenever you add code, Unity needs to compile it in the background. Note that any errors with the compilation itself will pop up on the bottom of your status bar.

Writing The Code

In the example I just showed you, there are a total of 2 methods. These are the Start and Update method, with the EnemyHP class getting its properties from the MonoBehavior class. This helps because you can then put it into any other GO.

There's a variety of methods that you'll use in your career; however, like with most programming languages, some things are often used, and others that are used fairly rarely. This is also the case with Unity, so here are the most common methods you'll use:

Start: The start method starts at the same time as the object comes into existence. This is to say that it begins in the 1st frame you put the GO in. This kicks into motion before any other method.

Awake: The awake method starts running whenever the object is initialized. It's worth noting that this doesn't mean all the GO's components have to be initialized at the same time. Whenever you start a MonoBehavior based class, you should use the Awake method, rather than using any other.

Update: The update method does exactly what it says on the tin. It updates the GO with whatever you need it to when certain requirements are fulfilled. It's best used when tracking and causing changes. This method will then keep running once a frame until it is stopped.

FixedUpdate: The FixedUpdate method is much like a more restricted version of the Update method. It calls a given number of times each second, regardless of what the framerate may be. This is usually used together with physics engines, so that lag doesn't cause unforeseen consequences.

```
// This will give you the first EnemyINT component that it finds
in the GO ( this is EnemyINT the component we are talking
about, not the GO.)\
var enemyINT =
GameObject.FindObjectOfType<EnemyINT>();
// We'll actually get a reference of its top-level GO.
var enemyGameObject = enemyINT.gameObject;

// If, instead, we want to know the enemi's current position, we
would do:
var position = enemyGameObject.transform.position;
```

Now then, you know how to find the enemy's position, as well as how to make it chase the hero. It's time for you to make a simple game on your own.

So, you will need to make four different kinds of objects for this game. The protagonist, the enemies, point spheres, and the powerup.

The protagonist should be able to move in all 4 directions using the WASD keys.

The game's goal will be for the protagonist to get to 100 points without the enemies catching up to him. Whenever they get a point sphere, their points should go up by 10.

The enemies will have a slightly smaller speed than the protagonist, and they will chase them throughout the game. Their sole purpose is simply to touch the protagonist. Once this happens, the protagonist either dies or loses one of their replenishing hearts (which could also be a pickup.) Now, which one of these two do you think is better game design?

The answer is: either

If you want a hardcore game, then make it so that any touch kills; if you want a more forgiving experience, then having refillable hearts or even a recharging HP gauge is the way to go. In this case, you could even give it a bit more of a strategic element by making the enemies disappear when they hit you.

The point spheres should spawn randomly across the map, and whenever a number of them spawn, you should add more enemies to the screen. This makes the game much more fun, as it makes the tensions and stakes rise the more points you collect.

The powerup will be a mechanic that allows you to either kill all the enemies on the screen currently or freeze them for a given duration.

Sounds simple, right? After you're finished with that game, I want you to think about it a bit. Consider how you could improve it and what you could do to it to make it more fun.

Moving On

If you choose to move on with Unity, you'll need a lot more than this. However, the material you've learned so far provides an excellent foundation not only in the building of your game itself but in the design aspect that is becoming increasingly more crucial in the era of visual editors.

Conclusion

This is it! We've come to the end of the road. If you feel like you've forgotten some, if not most of the material you've learned here, that's okay. Retaining even a bit of the information makes you a better game programmer than you were yesterday.

It's worth keeping in mind that this book is always there and that the design tips aren't made to be memorized; rather, you should always be ready to return to them and read them again.

Since the time you started this book, you've become a full-fledged game programmer. Now, I'm not saying you can go off and get a job at EA tomorrow; however, you have a foundation that's hard to beat.

From here on out, you can get to a vast variety of places and learn a lot of new things.

Let's recap what you've learned here, shall we?

The most important thing you've learned, in my opinion, is what to expect of the job.

There are far too many people that I've seen enter the industry and then leave due to burnout after they find out that they just aren't cut out for it. That they simply don't have the work ethic, the smarts, or the ability to sustain their interest and love for a project that they've just spent over 100 hours in a week working on.

Some people also enter the field, expecting it to be challenging 24/7. Like any other job, being a game programmer has its boring bits. I'm not going to sit here and tell you that I'm exhilarated whenever I have to program walking for the three thousandth time. With that being said, the job does have its perks, and that's why I love to do it.

You've also learned the ins and outs of AAA and indie development. This is a difference that many developers don't learn until it's too late in their careers to make the switch. Fortunately, you're in the position to make a choice for yourself immediately, rather than gambling on it without knowing.

Next, we went over Ruby. While we could've gone with a more complex language, Ruby has the beauty of being easily readable and is probably the easiest object-oriented programming language to learn. Despite it not being the most popular game development language.

Again, you might not use Ruby on the job, but if you need to learn Java or C++ for a job now, you'll find that it's no challenge at all; after all, you already know the most important principles, just under easier remembered names.

You also learned to use the Gosu game library in order to incorporate graphics into your games, as well as how to make simple multiplayer games like MUDs.

We went over RPG Maker, one of the best engines to let you understand how much work exactly goes into making a turn-based RPG. Every NPC, every shopkeeper, every ability has work that went into it.

Then we went into game design. All the programming in the world won't help you succeed if you don't understand how games work. At best, you'll be stuck in a dead-end position in a big company. Knowing how games work and how you can make them more fun is the easiest way to get a promotion in the game dev world.

Finally, you learned how to develop a simple game with Unity, a professional game engine. At this point, you can make your own serious projects.

The most important part I want you to take away from this book is the importance of experimentation. By experimenting with genres, with principles, with coding practices, you get much more knowledge than you would by reading off of a piece of paper.

I will now leave you with one of my favorite quotes out there by Leo Babauta:

"Rip off the greats, and the goods as well. Mimic and make it your own. Try to err."

www.ingramcontent.com/pod-product-compliance
Lightning Source LLC
LaVergne TN
LVHW022322060326
832902LV00020B/3608